Rent

What is Political Economy? series

Rent

Joe Collins

polity

First published in 2022 by Polity Press

Polity Press
65 Bridge Street
Cambridge CB2 1UR, UK

Polity Press
101 Station Landing
Suite 300
Medford, MA 02155, USA

ISBN-13: 978-1-5095-3905-5
ISBN-13: 978-1-5095-3906-2 (pb)

A catalogue record for this book is available from the British Library.

Library of Congress Control Number: 2021941064

Typeset in 10.5 on 12pt Sabon
by Fakenham Prepress Solutions, Fakenham, Norfolk NR21 8NL
Printed and bound in Great Britain by CPI Group (UK) Ltd, Croydon

The publisher has used its best endeavours to ensure that the URLs for external websites referred to in this book are correct and active at the time of going to press. However, the publisher has no responsibility for the websites and can make no guarantee that a site will remain live or that the content is or will remain appropriate.

Every effort has been made to trace all copyright holders, but if any have been overlooked the publisher will be pleased to include any necessary credits in any subsequent reprint or edition.

For further information on Polity, visit our website:
politybooks.com

For Kellie West

Contents

Acknowledgements

This short book was hard to write. So hard that it needed to be written twice. I am indebted to the many people who helped to transform a loose set of reflections on rent into what is hopefully a useful resource for demystifying capitalism with its rentier inflection.

Many thanks to George Owers and two anonymous readers for sharp and thorough comments on a chaotic first draft. Reader 2, who typically gets a bad rap, gets special mention for a fair and tough appraisal that continues to offer much food for thought. Thanks, also, to Julia Davies for patiently guiding a novice author through the publication process of his first book. Gail Ferguson's expert copyediting is much appreciated. So, too, is the professionalism of Evie Deavall, Sue Duncan, Neil de Cort and the rest of the Polity crew responsible for producing this book.

Sounding boards that helped shape thinking about rent over years are too many to name but chats with Beck Pearse, Humphrey McQueen, Claire Parfitt, Bruce McFarlane, Emma To, Peter Curtis, Liz Humphrys, Troy Henderson, Adam Morton, Frank Stilwell, Ben Moody, Franklin Obeng-Odoom, Bill Dunn, Chris Fletcher, Mike Beggs, Ryan Jory, Bill Kolios and Gareth Bryant directly informed the chapters below. Thank you, comrades. To the students and colleagues in the political economy movement at Sydney, your influence on the ideas in context explored in this book is immense and treasured.

The invisible work of many hands making and remaking our daily lives is so important and seldom acknowledged. To this end, I am grateful most of all to my family, Kellie, Matilda and Chips, for their unwavering support and encouragement without which this book could not have been written. Kellie, this book is dedicated to you because you more than anyone has helped me grapple with contradiction, class, land and value – the very essence of rent. I love you all and thank you for your patience and understanding during the struggle to finish this thing. Thanks, too, Bill, Amy, Julie, Dave, Kim, Mike, Taylor, Jamie, Jason, Jenny and Jimmy for all the help along the way.

It goes without saying that anything of use in what follows is owed to the collaborative efforts of those listed above while any errors of fact or interpretation are mine alone.

1
What is Rent?

The word 'rent' first appeared in English around the twelfth century. In this original usage, rent meant income received by landlords and paid by tenants for the use of land. The word probably came from the French *rente*, meaning income, derived from the Latin, *rendere*, meaning to give back or give up.[1] The word 'land' was used synonymously in this context with the things that could be done with land, like housing and farming. Rent was therefore taken to mean the periodical payment by tenants to landlords for the use of land and for what could be done on and with the land. One interesting connection is to the word 'farm', which meant 'payment as rent' in thirteenth-century English. Its Latin root is *firmare*, meaning 'to fix.'[2] There appear to be instances where the word 'rent' was used to mean tax in reference to various forms of property, but these were rare compared to the usage of the term to refer to the income derived from ownership of land. These discrepancies may well come down to the fact that in order for something to be given back, *rendere*, it first needed to be *rent*, torn apart, from its possessor. Rent as payment for the use of land remained its dominant meaning until the late nineteenth century.

It is around the 1880s that the word 'rent' begins to be used to refer to things besides land and its associated uses. Economists at this time begin to describe elements of the incomes of businesspeople as the 'rent of rare natural abilities', for example.[3] This shift in how rent is conceived, within the context of broader debates in economic theory, opens the door for expanding the list of things to which the word 'rent' can apply. Rent comes to bear on a raft of different types of 'property' from this time, making the meaning of rent more ambiguous.

More recent examples of rent conceived in this generalized form could include the periodical payment for housing or the fee paid for the temporary use of a car or some other piece of expensive machinery. People holidaying in Bali or Mykonos might well rent a motorized scooter rather than buying one because they require its use for the duration of their stay only. Purchasing a scooter might be prohibitively expensive, given it would be used solely for the purpose of commuting from their bungalow to the beach for a few weeks. The same might apply for the purchase of a gym membership in the months leading up to embarking on a beachside getaway. Monthly instalments are paid to use weights and treadmills rather than purchasing loads of expensive gym equipment that may well be neglected upon returning home from warmer climes.

Paying rent for housing is also a familiar experience for many today. The latest OECD data suggest that homeownership rates are high in most member countries, with 68% of people across the OECD owning homes either outright or with a mortgage, compared to 28% renting either privately or in subsidized housing.[4] There are two countries only, Switzerland (55%) and Germany (47%), where renting through the market is more common than homeownership.[5] The population of the OECD is around 1.3 billion people, according to latest figures, which is roughly 17% of the global population of around 7.6 billion people.[6] This means that about 364 million people living in OECD countries live in rented housing, almost one in every three people.

Recent increases in the renting population are also worth noting. The United Kingdom, for example, led the world between 2010 and 2015 in numbers of people becoming renters, with a 22% increase according to OECD figures.[7] The United States in comparison had 6.2 million people join the ranks of renters, with a 9.3% increase over the same period.[8] So while homeownership remains the dominant form of gaining access to housing on average in high-income countries, the rise in the renting population is significant and there are certainly enough of the population who do rent housing to make this form of rent a familiar arrangement for most people.

Just as with rents for scooters in Kuta, the rental payment for housing appears to be a relatively straightforward matter. A homeowner, or landlord, charges periodical fees, a rent, to those who require housing but do not own, or choose not to live in, a home of their own. The choice not to live in a home of one's own might seem strange but it does occur in places like the United Kingdom, the United States, Canada, Australia, Germany and Japan, where laws allowing investors to recoup losses on rental properties through income tax deductions make this choice profitable in some cases.[9] The conditions of the rental arrangement are usually set out in a tenancy contract whereby things like the amount of money to be paid for rent, how frequently this payment occurs, the length of the lease, the types of use permitted for the property and the rights of the tenants and landlord are spelled out in detail. This is why lawyers refer to 'contract rent'. Responsibilities of each party are set out in these contracts according to general principles that are fairly intuitive. Landlords, as owners of the property, are generally expected to ensure that it is fit for the purpose of habitation. In return, it is expected that renters do not destroy what is not theirs and that they leave the place in decent condition. But, just like the horror stories of tourists who have been duped by shonky operators in holiday destinations or caught out by the fine print in insurance policies, the housing rent issue is also more complicated than it might first seem.

The UK-based homeless charity Shelter conducted a tenant survey in August 2017 that found around a quarter of a million women in England had been offered the opportunity to substitute sex for rent in the previous five years, with 140,000 being propositioned in the previous year alone.[10] This survey prompted media reporting that brought some of the sordid details of these experiences to light. Evictions for refusing to have sex with landlords and the lowering of rent in exchange for sex are two examples.[11] Journalists went on to conduct undercover investigations, impersonating prospective tenants replying to advertisements posted by landlords online that used coded language to imply a sex-for-rent arrangement. More cases of sexual harassment were revealed by these investigations in both the United Kingdom in 2019[12] and by similar investigations in the United States in 2020.[13] In the case of the United States, a survey conducted in May 2020 by the National Fair Housing Alliance of more than a hundred fair housing organizations found that 13% registered an increase in complaints about sexual harassment since the start of the Covid-19 pandemic in March 2020.[14]

The executive director of the Hawaii State Commission on the Status of Women remarked in April 2020 that there had been more cases of sexual harassment of tenants by landlords reported in the last two weeks than in the previous two years.[15] Renee Williams, a staff attorney with the National Housing Law Project, said that 'landlords have all the leverage in the landlord–tenant relationship and in these types of situations they especially prey on women who are vulnerable, who are housing insecure, have bad credit or who don't have anywhere to go.' Williams went on to claim that 'We've already seen that the pandemic is exacerbating a lot of systemic issues and sexual harassment targeted at tenants by landlords is likely to be one of these issues.'[16]

Rent strikes are another example of systemic social issues flaring up during the pandemic. As the name suggests, rent strikes are coordinated refusals to pay rent with the aim of putting pressure on landlords to address problems to do with the rental arrangement. There were calls, for example, for coordinated rent strikes to begin on May Day 2020 across the United States, with catchcries like #CancelRent and #CantPayMay doing the rounds on social media.[17] Democratic Congressperson Alexandria Ocasio-Cortez publicly endorsed the proposal, claiming that 'People aren't striking because they don't feel like paying rent; they're striking because they can't pay rent.'[18] Organizers of the May Day rent strikes in New York claim that while rent strikes are usually aimed at getting landlords to improve conditions for tenants, these are intended to prod lawmakers into offering up rental assistance to renters struggling in the course of mass unemployment during the pandemic.[19] In the week prior to May Day, 3.8 million Americans became unemployed, joining the 30 million who had lost their jobs since the pandemic started.[20]

Across the Atlantic, rent strikes have been organized in London, Dublin, Barcelona, Madrid, Rome and Athens throughout 2020.[21] Mortgage holidays and a moratorium on evictions are some of the policy measures that have been implemented in the United Kingdom as a means to deal with mass unemployment in the midst of the pandemic. Even with these measures in place, there have been instances reported of eviction notices being served that come into effect as soon as the moratorium ends. Tenants of 170 privately rented apartments in Hackney, East London, were served eviction notices by their landlord, Simpson House 3 Limited, in June 2020. The mayor of Hackney, Philip Glanville, called them 'revenge evictions' that targeted tenants who had signed an open letter calling for rent decreases for those hit hardest by the pandemic job losses.[22] The billionaire property entrepreneur John Christodoulou has been identified as the key stakeholder behind the evictions and who is also the person responsible for funding the purchase of 75,000 care packages that have been delivered to the homeless and struggling families in the areas of London where his properties are located.[23]

University students have also coordinated rent strikes across the United Kingdom in late 2020. Their grievances include being treated as 'cash cows' by universities in the midst of a pandemic where in-person teaching and campus life is limited. Cambridge student Laura Hone claims the colleges 'are so rich they absolutely have the means to make rent cuts and ensure staff are not laid off . . . yet they continually put profit ahead of the welfare of students and staff'.[24] Hone went on to say that 'the education system should prioritize the welfare of students and staff, but universities are not going to come to this conclusion on their own. Students have to make them listen and rent is the most powerful leverage we have.'[25]

While the basis of housing rent is simply the fact that people require housing to live, and that those who do not own it must procure it, these examples demonstrate there is nothing simple about the matter. In the case of the sex-for-rent scandal, gendered violence and the power structures that facilitate it seem to be aggravated by the financial hardships caused by increasing unemployment during the pandemic. Those calling and organizing rent strikes are doing so out of desperation, facing the very real prospect of deteriorating living conditions due to the pressures of having to pay the rent. It is clear also that there are financial impera- tives constraining the benevolence of landlords, who might themselves be shackled to mortgages. The debtor, staring at an outstretched hand awaiting money they do not have, is probably not overly concerned about whether the appendage belongs to a financier or a rentier. What appears as a simple matter of payment for the use of housing is undergirded by several issues that extend beyond the individual actors to their societal context with very real and immediate conse- quences for all involved in the rental relationship.

While rent remains an income to landlords, it has also come to apply to lots of different types of property. Like any word, the meaning of 'rent' depends upon the context of its use. But unlike most other words, rent has become the subject of contention in economic theory, whereby its usage by those concerned with the subject matter of economics is loaded and requires some understanding of what is at stake in defining rent. Put simply, rent either must relate to land or it does not. Each leads to a different path for understanding what rent means today. This chapter is about working through some of these tensions, particularly in relation to this initial problem, of the relationship between rent and land. The next section looks at how and why rent is enjoying something of a renewal in interest across the social sciences and popular discourse.

Introducing the new '-ization' of the 2020s

If 'globalization' was the overarching process occupying social scientists in the 1990s, 'neo-liberalization' took that title in the noughties before being replaced by 'financialization' in the 2010s. So say critics of the scholarship on financialization. The discourse, some claim, has lost its conceptual coherence, becoming so fragmented that, 'to the degree that it is exces- sively vague and stretched, it is an increasingly nebulous and even, arguably, unhelpful signifier.'[26] Similar concerns about the usefulness of the concept of neo-liberalism have been raised by some who claim that 'the conceptual confusion outweighs the constructive debate around the term's meaning and that there is insufficient consensual core of shared understanding to justify keeping the term.'[27] In spite of these criticisms, or perhaps because of them, those urging caution for expanding studies of old descriptors for 'new' variants of capitalism are some of the loudest among the chorus of those advocating the next one – *rentierization.*[28]

Rentier capitalism is the latest stage of capitalism, according to this growing body of scholarship. To take one recent definition of the concept, rentier capitalism is a 'system of economic production and reproduction in which income is dominated by rents and economic life is dominated by rentiers'. This system is not just one dominated by rents and rentiers, it is 'in a much more profound sense, substantially scaffolded and organized around the assets that generate those rents and sustain those rentiers'.[29] Rent, according to this account, is 'payment to an economic actor (the rentier) who receives that rent – and this is the key factor – *purely by virtue of controlling something valuable*' (italics in the original).[30] This new variant differs from its predecessors in that capitalism is so named because it is, at least according to its devotees, driven by the entrepreneurial nous of capitalists, employing labour and resources to produce goods and services, profiting in the process so as to invest in further rounds of production, promoting growth of the system. This new rentier variant, whereby profits are increasingly taking the form of economic rents, is characterized by rentiers seeking to expand their asset portfolios in order to increase rents, without actually producing anything. Capitalism is meant to be about getting rich by *doing* things to make profits. Rentier capitalism is instead about getting rich by *having* things that create rents and then capturing them. Several books on the subject have been published in the last few years alone, with many more academic journal articles and journalistic pieces taking up associated themes, putting 'rentier capitalism' in prime position to become the social science buzzword of the 2020s.

It is in the context of this flurry of intellectual activity that the problem of rent has taken on renewed significance. The spectre of rentiers pocketing that which they did not earn is once again haunting the world. Their first appearance in the conventional story of capitalism was as wealthy landowners, reaping the rewards gifted by hereditary title while immiserated workers, shrewd industrialists and savvy merchants toiled to create a new social system that rewarded effort rather than accidents of birth. Their second coming, as monopolists of technology, minerals, housing and most other goods and services required to enjoy decent lives, is concerning, if, as the rentier capitalism literature suggests, today's economy is structured primarily to make it easier for them to get rich by holding what the rest of us want and need to ransom. Whether these claims stack up is, for now at least, beside the point. Such arguments have become so popular now that they set the tone and register for how people talk about current social problems. Topics like inequality, climate change, economic crisis and now even the causes and consequences of pandemics are increasingly linked to questions of rent in the popular imagination.[31] Think inheritance tax and inequality, resource rents and carbon emissions, the Google tax and fiscal crisis, and now also vaccine nationalism in response to the Covid-19 pandemic.

This is as much a welcome development as one that is cause for concern. Attempts to reveal how capitalism works in real time are required by those who want to understand society by changing it. But the conceptual coherence of the literature on rent is already fragmented, even before the discourse of rentier capitalism has had the opportunity to mushroom and mature as did those of globalization, neo-liberalism and financialization before it. The charge of conceptual confusion levelled at the scholarship of neo-liberalism and financialization refers to a period of decline in which the intellectual terrain has been exhausted after years of debate and analysis. It is precisely because of the proliferation of contradictory positions on these topics that the concepts themselves became incoherent. The rentier capitalism scholarship, however, begins from a place of conceptual confusion on rent. The contested nature of rent theory in capitalism has either been forgotten or neglected or has simply been obscured by the sheer volume of output from mainstream economics passing off its own understanding of rent as the only one available. Those laying the foundation for the critical analysis of capitalism with its rentier inflection have started to lay these tensions bare. They could use some help.

Opportunities remain for sharpening the contrast between and within the different strands of rent theory. Rentier capitalism studies demonstrate how systems of ownership, the relationships between people that they create and the potential for changing them are bound up in how rent is first understood. Whether rentier capitalism can be fixed and by what means depends on how exactly so-called rentier-ization happens. Conceptual coherence is required for these questions to be asked, let alone answered. Those building an explanation of rentier capitalism demonstrated why through their previous critiques of financialization, asking how useful is the term 'financialization' in explaining current changes in capitalism and if such a meta-concept was necessary at all. Similar lines of inquiry considered if the concept of neo-liberalism reproduces the very state/market binary it seeks to despatch and if the generality of the term and inconsistency in its use make it useful at all in identifying strategic priorities for left politics. It is crucial that rent theory is itself brought in for what critical theorists call immanent critique – deconstructing rent theory to strip it down to its building blocks and then reconstructing it to check for consistency, logic and contradictions – lest similar fault lines crop up in the logic of rentierization.

The stripping down and building back up of theories of rent frame the structure of what follows. This first chapter sets out brief preliminaries outlining the aim and structure of the immanent critique of rent theory for the purpose of shoring up the conceptual coherence of the emerging scholarship on rentier capitalism. A simple but important question informs the chapter: what is rent? After dealing with some basic elements of rent theory and the social phenomena it seeks to explain, chapter 2 situates rent theory in historical perspective, sketching out the context within which specific contributions to the historiography of rent were made and, most importantly, reflecting on how they helped change the societies under investigation. Key mainstream views and alternatives from political economy are then surveyed, identifying merits and limitations of each, using real-world examples in chapters 3 and 4. Chapter 5 considers the significance of rent theory today by looking closely at how rents are implicated in the social processes generating economic inequality, stalling economic dynamism in global capitalism and the climate crisis. Specific episodes are examined with a view to spotlighting the role of rents in generating circumstances for what have come to be known as globalization, neo-liberalism and financialization. The discussion in this final chapter is concerned mainly with why and how the study of rent is important going forward.

That takes care of the 'why' and the 'what' questions. How will the critique of rent theory proceed? While penning the introduction to the third volume of *Capital* after painstakingly assembling the manuscript from his dead friend's mountains of chicken-scrawled notes, Frederick Engels made the comment that 'where things and their mutual relations are conceived not as fixed but rather as changing, their mental images, too, i.e. concepts, are also subject to change and reformulation.' Such phenomena, Engels argues, are 'not to be encapsulated in rigid definitions, but rather developed in their process of historical or logical formation'.[32]

A little under a century later, Ben Fine dispensed the following scholarly rebuke of a pivotal contribution to mainstream rent theory by Joseph Buchanan. Fine contends that the 'doctrines of the past should not be seen as an evolutionary approach to those of the present,' but rather, 'different theories utilise different concepts and theoretical frameworks as well as posing different questions, ones that may not be posed let alone answerable within another theory'.[33] This is, Fine notes, 'a popular but misguided method of approach to the history of economic thought, or indeed to the history of any discipline'.[34]

The crux of both statements might seem like common sense, but it never ceases to amaze how some economic writing seems to lose sight of what most reasonable people would consider uncontroversial – things change, so our ideas for understanding them should too, and the different ways we make sense of our complex reality in motion cannot all be understood from a single perspective. It is on the basis of this sound advice that the inquiry into the character, causes and consequences of rent proceeds.

The contested meaning of rent: land or monopoly?

Rent is one revenue among a few in economic theory that designates flows of value through society. Wages, interest and profit are others. The task of rent theory is not only to track the direction and magnitude of rental flows, but also to understand how they came about, the consequences of where they go and also why it is they exist at all in any given society. As will be shown below, there are lots of different ways people have emphasized aspects of these questions and called them 'rents'. One challenge when making sense of these different perspectives is to decide on what basis to make separations, or comparisons, between them. One way is to split the contending views on rent along the axis of what rent theory is really all about – land or monopoly?

There are two broad orientations when it comes to theories of rent. One suggests that rent is essentially about monopoly. To put it another way, a concept of rent is helpful insofar as it tells us something about how markets function, or perhaps how a dysfunctional market might operate. This view accepts that all things are scarce when considered relative to their demand. It is therefore how this scarcity is mediated by the different claims people have over property that determines the flows and levels of rents. As with the example of housing above, rent explained from this perspective could be understood as the income received by the owners of scarce goods. The one in three people in the OECD, for example, who rent housing do so, it could be argued, because housing stock is too expensive for them to buy. The price of this housing stock could be explained by demand exceeding supply and therefore the scarcity of housing stock is what pushes prices of houses up and compels people to rent.

The second orientation in rent theory suggests that rent should be conceived only as the revenue that owners of land receive for permitting its use. There are contending views within this approach as to what exactly the rents are paid for, how the levels of rent are determined and why they exist, but there is an insistence overall that rent theory is principally about understanding the role of land in the economy.

The housing example explained from this perspective might argue that it is because land itself is scarce, in absolute terms, that the price of housing is driven up to the point that a third of the OECD population is forced to rent. This line of argument is still concerned with scarcity but only as it is a characteristic unique to land. Another tack, still within the land-based orientation, might claim that it is not just the finite nature of land that drives rents, but rent is also about the ways in which land is owned, rather than the fact that land can be owned. In countries where land ownership and control is split among various stakeholders, for example, the different groups who hold titles to different plots of land may well affect the pricing of housing stock. Explanations for why Germany and Switzerland are outliers when it comes to the numbers of renters compared to homeowners might look towards the historical development of land ownership in these countries or the ways in which their governments have historically acted to affect housing supply in relation to demand.

Figure 1.1 sketches a very basic map of how these views connect. The land/monopoly dichotomy is not exactly neat. Some who claim that rent is primarily about monopoly also believe that it should be considered a revenue specific to owners of land. Indeed, those who have taken the view that rent is about monopoly have produced important work on the subject, examining the various ways in which rents have materialized in modern political economies and the

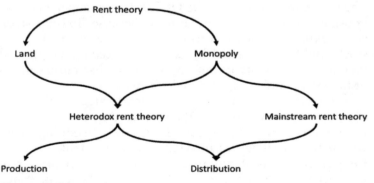

Figure 1.1

role they play in either facilitating or mitigating economic development. This map of sorts is not meant to be detailed but rather it indicates a key distinction in rent theory debates, to be layered upon other differences explored in the next few chapters. The starting point could just have easily been different schools of thought or indeed the key theorists associated with developments in thinking about rent. The current framing was chosen to emphasize the important role that considerations of land have played in the historical debates on rent theory.

This chapter has offered preliminaries on the meaning of rent, its ongoing significance in social science and how we might make sense of the term today. Its key points relate to the contested meaning of rent in recent history and what this ambiguity might mean for current studies of capitalism with its rentier inflection. The most familiar form of rent, that paid for housing, was examined briefly to demonstrate that what appears to be a fairly simple matter of payment for the temporary use of a basic need is much more interesting and complicated. The next chapter deals with the history of economic thought as it relates to rent theory.

2

Rent Theory in Historical Perspective

Changes in rent theory have tended to reflect broader developments in the history of economic thought. This chapter discusses some of these developments, why they occurred and how they inform current debates on rent. The connection emphasized in this chapter is between historically specific theories of rent and the social context in which they emerged and came to change.

Rent before capitalism

In the long and relatively obscure history of Islamic economic thought, at least for audiences in the Anglophone countries, there are important contributions to rent theory worth noting. Abu Yousuf, who lived between 731 and 798, advocated a proportionate rent in kind rather than levying a fixed rent on agricultural land. The rationale was that charging a rent proportionate to the output of the land would incentivize expanded production, whereas a fixed rent might stifle expansion.[1] Yousuf's work on principles of taxation is thought to have pre-empted the 'canons of taxation' – equity, certainty, convenience and economy – that emerged in the work of the classical school of political economy from Adam Smith onwards.[2] Abu Muhammad bin Hazm, who died in 1064, was a jurist concerned with the collective responsibilities of the state. Ibn Hazm was unique among the four schools of Islamic jurisprudence as an advocate for prohibition of renting out of agricultural land, favouring that owners cultivate the land themselves or enter into share-cropping arrangements. Support for this policy of prohibition of renting has been labelled as socialistic by some, and it is widely considered to be in opposition to the mainstream of Islamic jurisprudence that permits the renting of agricultural land.[3]

Medieval economic thought of Western Europe offered the following contributions to rent theory. Economies in the later Middle Ages, from the twelfth to fifteenth centuries, in Western Europe were characterized as regional, wherein each town or region was serviced by a surrounding agricultural district. Production and exchange took place primarily within the region, within and between town and country. Peasants represented the majority and they produced mainly for their own subsistence. Anything extra was distributed upwards among the various social groups. Lords presided over the regions and they received what was called a 'quickrent' in the form of surplus food produced on peasant land in return for permitting peasants to live and subsist on the lord's estates.[4] This is where the term 'landlord' originates. The lord's own manor, or residence, also had a tillage where produce for the manor was grown and peasants were required to perform compulsory labour on this tillage. This labour that peasants performed for the lord was known as the *barshchina* or *corvée*.[5]

It is tempting to say that these are examples of land rent, or labour rent, in the case of the *corvée*, but that would remove these examples of rent from their historical context. Deriving ahistorical definitions of rent and then imposing them on any example that fits the abstract definition is the kind of folly that Fine warned against in chapter 1. Doing so would obscure the fact that the society in which this 'rent', the *corvée*, was being paid had a different form of social organization from society today. This means that our preju-dices and views of how the world functions are transported back to the period under observation, effectively reproducing our society in theirs. The level of rent in the late medieval period, for example, is not determined by the degree of market power in markets for factors of production. The idea of a labour market as we understand it today in the context of that society is simply ridiculous. Indeed, the construct of a 'market' itself, with buyers and sellers free to enter apparently mutually beneficial relations of exchange mediated by some form of generally accepted and guaranteed currency, is completely nonsensical in a time when people were effectively enslaved by despots whose social power ostensibly derived from divine providence.

The crucial connection between production and distribution, mediated by agricultural production, was seen clearly by scholars of political economy in the Confucian period in the history of Chinese economic thought. *Shi*, or food production, was considered the foremost issue for ruling a country by Confucius amidst the need for weapons and the confidence of the people in their ruler.[6] The policy of 'light tax' was preferred to stimulate an increase in production by keeping the rental payment for the use of farmland paid by farmers to landowners at a rate that did not disincentivize taking more land under cultivation. The rationale for this approach to rent and taxation was expressed clearly by one of the students of Confucius, You Ruo, who adduced that 'when the people enjoy plenty, the prince necessarily shares in that plenty' but when 'the people have not enough for their needs, the prince cannot expect to have enough for his needs'.[7]

Theories of rent in pre-capitalist societies were chiefly concerned with how exactly to facilitate the production and distribution of food. Rents conveyed the economic aspect of problems associated with land ownership. The measures of rent or their equivalences were expressed in forms other than the money payment that is taken for granted today because the monetary economy was not yet widespread. Perhaps the division of labour in these societies did not necessitate a universal equivalent form, something that could facilitate exchange throughout a complex economy where the sheer volume of commodities and their types required something other than exchange in kind. It took the explosion in productive capacity in agriculture that emerged in capitalism to displace the rent problem into other spheres of economic activity where ownership and the imperative to benefit from controlling access to productive resources became a source of enrichment.

Physiocracy and landed property in capitalism

Physiocracy means rule of nature. The term was coined by Pierre-Samuel du Pont de Nemours in 1767 to describe the work of François Quesnay and Victor Riqueti, Marquis de Mirabeau.[8] Quesnay transformed economics from the study of managing households, cities and states, which was its original designation in ancient Greece as *oikonomia*, to the science of wealth.[9] The physiocrats were responsible for disengaging the 'economic process from its anthropological role as servant of the socio-political order, and established its claim to be the direct manifestation of the natural order', or, in other words, they argued that 'economic process itself embodied natural law and should thus dictate the socio-political order.'[10] The stated aim of physiocracy was to 'attain to the greatest degree of prosperity possible for society' in accordance with the 'general laws of the natural order'.[11] This initiative led them to inquire as to the origins of value, its distribution and the consequences of these movements. Results of these investigations were important contributions to an evolving social science of political economy. This group of French scholars can be grouped together, for our current purposes, with British scholars such as John Law, William Petty, Richard Cantillon, David Hume, James Steuart, Dudley North and John Locke. French and English traditions of political economy find a degree of unity in the work of Adam Smith, forming the foundation of what is now considered the school of classical political economy.

Smith wove various threads spun by these thinkers to shift the focus from exchange, underpinning the mercantilist writing of people like Thomas Mun and Jean-Baptiste Colbert, to production and to question the primacy of land as the driver of economic activity and as the source of value. Anything before Smith in European economic thought can be taken together in relation to rent theory, so physiocracy will act as a proxy uniting what is a diverse group of thinkers. The physiocratic theory of rent is emphasized to discuss the shift in thinking evident in economic theories of the time attempting to explain the disintegration of feudalism and the emergence of capitalism.

Qesnay, Mirabeau and Anne Robert Jacques Turgot are the key figures associated with physiocracy. Qesnay's skilful use of the systems of patronage saw him elevated to an influential position within the court from which his economic theories came to dominate the French tradition of economics.[12] The foundation for the system of thought that would become known as physiocracy was laid with the publication of Qesnay's *Tableau Économique* (Economic Tables) in 1758. The etymology of the term traces from the Greek *physis*, nature, and *kratein*, to rule. Turgot's *Réflexions sur la Formation et la Distribution des Riches* (Reflections on the Formation and Distribution of Riches), published in 1770, expressed this sentiment clearly with the statement that the earth 'is always the first and only source of wealth; it is that which as the result of cultivation produces all the revenue; it is that also which has provided the first fund of advances prior to all cultivation'.[13]

The theory of value elaborated by the physiocrats meant that rent was integral to their system of political economy. This school is credited with affecting the pivotal shift within economic thought that helped craft the tax regimes that drove the French peasants to revolution.[14] Whereas mercantilists thought that value was produced through exchange, the physiocrats, along with their British counterparts, considered value derived from the process of material production. In so doing, the physiocrats contributed to laying the foundations for an analysis of capitalism. As another pioneering critic of capitalism notes, 'The Physiocrats transferred the inquiry into the origins of surplus value from the sphere of circulation into the sphere of direct production, and thereby laid the foundation for the analysis of capitalist production.'[15]

The main limitation of physiocratic economic theory was an underdeveloped conception of exchange value. This lopsidedness meant that use value was perceived as the only form of value, which, in turn, obscured the real nature of value production outside of agriculture. We can consider use value simply as the value attributed to the use of something and exchange value as the value for which something is exchanged. The use value of a meal, for example, is gleaned in its nutrition and tastiness, whereas its exchange value might be measured in how much it costs. From the vantage point of use value alone, it is hard to avoid the conclusion that farm labourers produce a surplus by virtue of consuming less than they grow. The production of a surplus in the processing of raw materials mediated by a system of exchanging commodities requires a theory of exchange value. The physiocrats, equipped with rudimentary conceptions of exchange value, could only see the creation of surplus arising in branches of industry where it is most clearly evident that consumption is less than production.

No wonder they thought 'agricultural labour is the only productive labour, because it is the only labour that produces a surplus-value, and rent is the only form of surplus-value.'[16] Such a view had two important implications: landowners, by virtue of their capacity to appropriate rent, were the most powerful class in society; however, landowners were also an unproductive, or sterile, social class. This insight provides the basis for both the construction of theories of value based on labour and a political campaign against the sterile class of landed proprietors, representing the last vestiges of feudal society. The consequence of physiocratic theory in practice was the opening of a line of argument against landowners, which had the important result of legitimizing the emerging social function of capitalists. In retrospect, it appears that the physiocrats deserve a high place amongst those who prepared the ideological grounds for the French Revolution.[17]

Material factors compelled the physiocrats to investigate the determinants of economic activity in their implications for French society. The relative backwardness of manufacturing and agriculture in France compared to British industry was key. Agricultural production was characterized by intensive peasant farming and sharecropping, with much of the proceeds going to absentee landlords. This situation was aggravated by the imposition of various taxes, like a grain export tax, used to fund a series of disastrous wars and the extravagance of the court.[18] Revolts became chronic among the peasantry.[19] These pressing concerns forced the physiocrats to confront the economic problems posed by the emergence of capitalism within the context of failed attempts to reimpose feudal dues and obligations.

Classical political economy and the class war on rentiers

The physiocratic theory of rent followed logically from their theory of value, which attributed its source to nature. By contrast, the British/Scottish classical school identified labour, rather than land, as the source and measure of value. The material development within an emerging capitalism that prompted this theoretical advance was the evidently increasing accumulation of capital. Capital in the register of classical political economy does not necessarily mean money but rather anything that can be considered useful in the production of goods and services that can be sold for profit. As capitalism penetrated further into English agriculture, the division of labour in society came more and more to resemble the structure of agricultural industry today, wherein a tenant farmer would employ labourers to work land leased from a landlord. This new way of organizing production in agriculture gave rise to political problems such as rising prices for agricultural goods in the face of rising demand. While the physiocrats opened a line of inquiry that questioned the social utility of what they called the 'sterile class' of landowners, classical political economists, with a few important exceptions, pursued with rigour the theoretical justification for eroding the economic and political power of the landed interest in favour of the emerging class of bourgeois industrialists.

The quantum shift in capital accumulation occurred throughout a period which has been, perhaps unhelpfully, referred to as when the 'Industrial Revolution' confronted a barrier in the form of a system of landed property in Britain. The demand for food required a reorganization of food production in Britain, while leaps and bounds occurred in the centralization and concentration of money, people, raw materials and machinery that churned the increase in the production of commodities. The workers required to furnish this growth congregated in urban centres owing to their dispossession from the countryside in the enclosures of common lands, occurring since about the fourteenth century. New conditions of production meant that people found themselves relating to others in ways hitherto unknown. Landlords still owned the land, but they found themselves confronting capitalist tenant farmers and farm labourers instead of peasants. These new class tensions in agricultural industry became the focal point of novel political issues.

Capitalism rationalizes industry because competition compels it. This rationalization process requires that land ownership as an institution is removed, or that its pernicious effects are at least resisted, because it poses a barrier to further investment of capital. The site of this conflict in nineteenth-century Britain was the Corn Laws debates. The physiocrats witnessed the primary stages of capitalism emerging in Europe. Their inquiries into the source of wealth paved the way for the construction of a theory of value in a maturing capitalism. The classical school, through their reconceptualization of class relations, grappled with the problems of capitalism as they emerged. These important changes in rent theory will now be examined in conjunction with the material developments that gave rise to them.

The first innovator of physiocratic rent theory was Adam Smith, who brought together the progress of English economic thought from the late mercantilist period and the substance of the school of physiocracy at the height of the Scottish Enlightenment.[20] Smith provided a bridge between physiocratic notions of rent and the Ricardian schema which made coherent the dynamics of capitalism as it emerged. Importantly, Smith emphasized the significance of landed property, or the institution whereby ownership of land is mediated, in his theory of rent. Ricardo would later expunge this vital function. What has been understood by many as incoherence in Smith's rent theory regarding the relation between rent and price is actually the articulation of a complex problem expressing a conjunctural class antagonism. This problem will now be elaborated by examining the physiocratic elements in Smith's theory of rent and the foreshadowing of Ricardian propositions.

It is not surprising Smith's rent theory is heavily influenced by the physiocrats. Smith visited France a decade before the publication of his famous *The Wealth of Nations* and was in direct, albeit infrequent, correspondence with important physiocrats such as Mercier de la Rivière, Nicolas

Baudeau and Anne Robert Jacques Turgot. It appears likely, though, that Smith's dependence on the physiocrats has been exaggerated and that they learned as much from him as he apparently incorporated from them into his books.[21] The area that does retain a significant element of physiocratic thought is Smith's theory of rent.

The economic system according to physiocracy was premised on the claim that nature was the source of value. Agricultural labour was therefore counterposed by non-agricultural labour in the social division of labour. This dichotomy was at the root of physiocratic thought. On this basis, they conflated profits and wages because, while they may have been genuinely separate categories, they became lumped together as against rent. This element of physiocracy, of the primacy of land over labour and capital taken together, appears in Smith's theory of rent, as the following excerpt from *The Wealth of Nations* demonstrates:

> It is the work of nature which remains after deducting or compensating everything which can be regarded as the work of man. It is seldom less than a fourth, and frequently more than a third of the whole produce. No equal quantity of productive labour employed in manufactures can ever occasion so great a reproduction. In them nature does nothing; man does all; and the reproduction must always be in proportion to the strength of the agents that occasion it.[22]

The notion that some element of surplus produce in agriculture is owed to nature rather than labour is physiocratic. While Smith is appropriately regarded as a pioneer of theories of value that emphasized labour as their source, his theoretical framework was clearly imbued with important aspects of physiocracy. What is the significance of this inheritance for Smith's theory of rent?

If land was the source of value for the physiocrats, rent was the form of surplus value that was then distributed in the form of revenues such as wages and profits. This is the reason the physiocrats and Smith required a theory of landed property. Such was the political power of landowners at the time that Smith could scarcely ignore the economic significance of the barrier they could pose to the spread of industry into agriculture and mining. As the changes now readily associated with the so-called Industrial Revolution began to accelerate into the nineteenth century, the power and influence of landowners became a fetter to the rational development of industrial agriculture and mining. By the time David Ricardo published his *Principles of Political Economy and Taxation* in 1817, detailing an alternative conception of rent and value to Smith's, the need for a theory of landed property, the economic concept explaining the social power of landowners, was being questioned alongside the need for the class of people it related to. This tension in theory was borne out in practice through the debates on the Corn Laws from 1815 to 1846.

The Corn Laws debates are an insight to the struggle between an emerging class of industrialists and landowners in nineteenth-century Britain. This antagonism had become so pronounced that by 1832 it dominated politics. To give a flavour of the dispute, consider the testimony of a commentator sympathetic to landowners:

> To those, therefore, who are in search of arguments for the purpose of supporting the partial views of either side, which have hitherto prevailed, I can hold out no encouragement to take the trouble of perusing the following pages: they will not find one single word declaiming landlords as selfish, monopolizing law-makers, or the manufacturers as sordid avaricious beings, grasping at the riches of the great, and treading on the rights of the poor: the subject has already been handled too much in this way.[23]

Whatever Wilson's motives, the Corn Laws were commonly perceived as the struggle between an emergent class of industrialists and the established, albeit declining, stratum of landowners. Hindsight has dulled the edges of these debates, and they are seen in the present period as the basis upon which modern liberal trade theory was settled. Ricardo's contribution to the debates, for example, are considered to have provided a calculating rationality to offset the false dichotomy of 'defense and opulence' presented by defenders of landowners like Reverend Malthus.[24] However, the consequences of this debate ramify into the present. Class tensions between industrialists and landowners were central to the removal of the corn tariff. A brief survey of key contributions to the debate will suffice to demonstrate that the theory of rent that emerged out of classical political economy reflects the class tensions that erupted in the Corn Laws debates.

Ricardo considered rent to be 'that portion of the produce of the earth which is paid to the landlord for the use of the original and indestructible powers of the soil'.[25] Mines, as well as land, Ricardo explained, 'generally pay a rent to their owner; and this rent, as well as the rent of the land, is the effect and never the cause of the high value of their produce'.[26] Rent is inherently a matter of comparative efficiency or advantage in this schema. If, claims Ricardo, 'there were an abundance of fertile mines, which anyone might appropriate, they could yield no rent; the value of their produce would depend on the quantity of labour necessary to extract the metal from the mine and bring it to market'.[27] Three elements of the classical theory of rent are presented here:

1 Rent is the portion of gains from production that is paid by industry to landowners. This distinction is decisive for Ricardo: 'It [i.e. rent] is often, however, confounded with the interest and profit of capital.'[28]
2 Rent is the effect rather than the cause of the value of produce. This means that for Ricardo, rent does not create value but rather is the result of the productive process that is the outcome of human labour. In accordance with his theory of value, often referred to as 'the labour theory of value', 'the value of a commodity, or the quantity of any other commodity for which it will exchange, depends on the relative quantity of labour which is necessary for its production, and not on the greater or lesser compensation which is paid for that labour.'[29]
3 The value of commodities produced in land-based industry is determined by the quantity of labour required to produce these commodities, leaving rent as a component factor of this final value to be realized through the exchange of

commodities in the market. Rent must be conceived as that unique element of surplus value of commodities gleaned from the exploitation of nature but is still ever constituted by the application of human labour.

Thomas Robert Malthus was another pioneer of classical political economy and one of Ricardo's contemporaries. Malthus defined rent as that 'portion of the value of the whole produce which remains to the owner of the land, after all outgoings belonging to its cultivation, of whatever kind, have been paid, including the profits of the capital employed, estimated according to the usual and ordinary rate of the profits of agricultural capital at the time being'.[30] Like Ricardo, Malthus distinguished rent from profits of capital and all other outgoing costs associated with the cultivation or production of commodities. Examples of such costs are labour, machinery and materials such as fertilizers or infrastructure like canals or irrigation. Both Malthus and Ricardo emphasize the distinction between such costs outlaid in the production process, the profits realized from the sale of goods produced and the rent paid to landowners for the right to exploit the finite resource of land and its appurtenances. Rent is therefore a component factor of the value of commodities whose production requires the use of specific areas of land. It is then only in land-based industry, where things like roads, canals, water and rail are vital, that rent is a concern.

John Stuart Mill referred to the so-called law of Ricardian rent as the *pons asinorum* of economics.[31] The literal meaning of *pons asinorum* is 'bridge of donkeys', referring to Euclid's maxim in geometry stating that the angles opposite the equal sides of an isosceles triangle are equal. Mill, it seemed, held Ricardo's concept of rent in the very highest regard. Mill came to prominence after Ricardo and Malthus died in 1823 and 1834, respectively. While heavily influenced by their work, Mill was not privy to the contemporaneous engagement enjoyed by Ricardo and Malthus in their lifetimes. In Mill's estimation, 'the requisites of production being labour, capital, and natural agents; the only person, besides the labourer and the capitalist, whose consent is necessary to production, and who can claim a share of the produce as the price of that consent, is the person who, by the arrangements of society, possesses exclusive power over some natural agent.'[32] Just as Ricardo and Malthus, Mill distinguishes the landowner from the labourer and the capitalist on the basis of owning nature.

Importantly, for Mill, the natural agent is unique but still just a component of the broader process of production so that 'land is the principal of the natural agents which are capable of being appropriated, and the consideration paid for its use is called rent.'[33] Moreover, landowners as a social class are special because they alone have a claim to a share of the surplus realized in the distribution of the produce, 'through ownership of something which neither they nor anyone else have produced'.[34] While the capitalist contributes capital and the labourer their labour, the landowner permits the right to exploit natural agents. Scarce resources are monopolized regardless of whether their owners actively conspire to that end; however, even when monopolized, 'a thing which is the gift of nature, and requires no labour or outlay as the conditions of its existence, will, if there be competition among the holders of it, command a price, only if it exists in less quantity than the demand.'[35] 'Natural agents', then, as a requisite of production, despite being devoid of value in the sense that Ricardo has defined in terms of the labour theory of value, still command a price when demand in society exceeds the available supply.

Rent exists not because variations in nature exist but because owners are able to control access to nature. Fertile land is finite and relatively scarce when taken in contrast to barren land. Ownership of fertile land therefore permits the landowner to impose a cost upon those who wish to exploit its bounty. The land itself seems possessed of the power to yield rent by virtue of its variegated ability to produce a surplus. As Mill contends, 'the power of such land to yield rent is exactly proportioned to its natural or acquired fertility, or to the general surplus which it can be made to produce beyond what is strictly necessary to support the labour and keep up the capital employed upon it.'[36]

The key distinction between Smith's theory of rent and those of Ricardo, Malthus and Mill is the role played by landed property. Smith permits landed property to obstruct the flow of capital because of the existence of physiocratic elements within his theory of value. Rent, for Smith, arises out of the obstacle posed by landed property for the application of capital to land. For Ricardo, rent arises from natural differences in the land itself. Rent is a product of the land rather than the class relation between landowners and capitalists. It is upon this basis that landed property is expunged from rent theory within the classical school of political economy.

Marx's 'shitty rent business'

In a letter to his friend and collaborator, Frederick Engels, dated 18 June 1862, Karl Marx quipped that he had at last been able to sort out the 'shitty rent business' – having long harboured misgivings as to the absolute correctness of Ricardo's theory, he had 'at length got to the bottom of the swindle'.[37] The swindle, explains Marx in another letter to Engels dated 2 August, is that Ricardo confused value and cost price, leading him to deny the existence of rent that was independent of variations in the fertility of the soil – i.e., Ricardo's differential rent outlined above.[38]

Marx's theory of rent is really an attempt to understand capitalist landed property. Rent, for Marx, was the economic form of a relationship between social classes. Just as wages express the class struggle between workers and bosses, or proletarians and bourgeoisie, rent was the tangible medium through which the scrap between landowners and capitalists could be observed. It is tempting to say, then, that Marx's theory might have been relevant in the 1860s but is clearly not today because a distinct class of landowners, pitched against capitalists and workers, like aristocrats of the feudal era, no longer exists. Indeed, many do take this position and therefore treat Marx's rent theory as an artefact to be revered with nostalgia but not to be taken seriously in a modern context. Others, however, reckon that what Marx theorized as the potential for conflict over surplus value – most commonly observed as profit in the register of popular economics today – between landowners and capitalists is in fact a problem unique to capitalism and one that not only persists to this day but is more pronounced than ever. What if, for example, the old landlord class were either bought out or became capitalists themselves, but the splitting up of profits between those who own land and those who put people and machines to work on it requires an understanding of rent, that the one Marx established is uniquely placed to explain? Or, to put it another way, what can Marx's theorization of rent tell us about landed property and capital accumulation in the twenty-first century?

Marx did the bulk of his work on rent in the early 1860s. This was at least a decade before the emergence of marginalist, or neoclassical, rent theory so it was not at all concerned with distinguishing between rent which emphasized a connection to land and rent which applied to all factors of production in the context of monopoly. Rent, for Marx, was a payment for the use of land. Indeed, the sections of *Capital* and the *Theories of Surplus Value* that deal with rent, about 600 pages in total, discuss 'ground rent'. The substantive section in volume 3 of *Capital,* is called the 'transformation of surplus profit into ground-rent'. Land, or, more specifically, how land was transformed into property in capitalism – i.e., landed property – was not just one area of focus for the study of rent, as with neoclassical rent theory, but rather its inextricable material basis.

This work generated three concepts through which a distinct theory of rent cohered: differential ground rent type 1 (DR1); differential ground rent type 2 (DR2); and absolute ground rent (AR). It is important to note that these concepts are mutually dependent and inseparable when considered in the real world, even if they can and must be taken independently for the purpose of analysis and exposition. We can explain them one at a time but in the real world they exist simultaneously and affect one another. Marx's rent theory is not about an accounting exercise where we just add up the three types of rent. Each is the material basis of the next, like a staircase. To take the point further, DR2 may well be understood on its own terms but it cannot exist without DR1, or outside the influence of AR and its effect on the social determination of productivity in agriculture.

DR1 concerns the differing productivity in agriculture as a function of competition between firms in the agricultural sector of the economy. The material basis of this differing productivity is the variation in quality of the land itself.

Imagine a stretch of the floodplain of the Nile River in Egypt. Plots of farmland closest to the water have the richest fertility of the soil owing to the proximity to water and to the seasonal replenishment of soil nutrients due to the ebb and flow of the tide. More crops would grow on land closer to the river and therefore the profits from cultivation on those plots would be greater than profits on farms further away from the river. Profitability would be highest close to the river and would decline as you moved further out. There would come a point where no profit could be made from cultivating land any further from the river because there was not enough demand for agricultural goods to cover the expenses of cultivation as well as for a profit margin more than the average for farming to incentivize investment. This point would be the limit of DR1. This concept appears to work in a similar way to Ricardo's notion of rent at the extensive margin.

DR2 is about the differing applications of capital to lands of equal fertility. Imagine there is an area of the Nile floodplain where all land is of equal fertility, accessing the same amount of water and being replenished with soil nutrients at the same rate. The factor determining rents in this group of plots would be the differing amounts of capital invested. If, for example, two farmers with plots side by side of equal fertility decided to install different watering techniques to water their wheat crops – one using cheap canals and the other using expensive mechanical sprinklers – whoever produced more would be said to be appropriating DR2 in the price of their goods. If farmer 1 with the canals produced 10,000 kilos of wheat per month, whereas farmer 2 with the sprinklers produced 15,000 kilos of wheat per month, then the level of DR2 would be 5,000 kilos of wheat. The important point to note about DR2 is that for the duration of the lease it is the capitalist farmer who reaps the rewards of the investment of capital into sprinklers but, once the lease is finished, the landowner would increase the rent by the level of increased productivity – i.e., the monetary value of 5,000 kilos of wheat. The farmer would have to pay this increased rent because they cannot continue to produce wheat without access to the land. The point therefore is that because land is property under capitalism and can be owned by someone, the incentive to invest in the increase of productivity is stifled.

How exactly productivity is affected depends upon the way in which the land is owned. In manufacturing, for example, the returns from extra investment that resulted in increased productivity would go to the investor, the capitalist. In agriculture, however, this surplus profit goes to the capitalist farmer initially, for the duration of the lease in which the investment is made, but it then goes to the landowner in subsequent leases as an increase in the rental fee for access to the land.

AR is different from both DR1 and DR2. Whereas DR (1 and 2) provides a way to understand the causes and consequences of productivity in agricultural industry, AR can explain the relationship of the rates of change of productivity between agriculture and other sectors of industry in the economy. Both DR and AR provide a means to understand the way that private ownership of land in capitalism – i.e., capitalist landed property – affects the way capitalism evolves. The formation of DR is driven by the determination of value and surplus profit in agriculture, whereas AR is contingent upon the transformation of market values into prices of production. These terms are unfamiliar to the mainstream discourse because Marx's concepts are derived from a different frame of reference, or epistemic community. A brief digression is required to flesh out what these terms mean to grasp the intuition behind the technical definition of AR – i.e., $AR = V - P$, where absolute ground rent equals the value of commodities produced in agriculture minus their prices of production.

A distinction needs to be made between value and price when dealing with economic theory prior to the 1870s. From that point onwards, the rise of neoclassical economics as the mainstream perspective means that value and price become conflated so that the price of something is also its value. In the epistemic frameworks of classical political economy and in Marx's critique of that approach, value is a contested category distinct from price. Value for Marx is abstract labour measured as socially necessary labour time. The determination of value occurs in the context of capital accumulation, in which spheres of production, distribution and exchange are united in a conjoined series of processes driven by the capacity for workers to create surplus value.

Price expresses value in the context of markets for commodities, its level oscillating around value in relation to supply and demand. Or, in Marx's words, value is the 'centre of gravity around which the prices of commodities fluctuate'.[39] Value is measured and expressed in terms of capital, whereas price is captured through revenues. The organic composition of capital (OCC), for example, is a concept that expresses the relationship between constant capital and variable capital. Constant capital is something involved in the production process that merely passes on its value to the commodity without adding more, hence its constancy. Variable capital is the component of capital involved in production that can vary, adding more value than existed at the start of production, thereby creating surplus value. These concepts are mental images of value relations that use capital to illuminate the flows of value in its process of self-expansion.

Such categories are distinct from those found in more familiar discussions of price theory. Variable capital, for example, can be understood concretely as capital advanced to pay the wages of workers involved in production. Wages are revenue paid to workers by capitalists in exchange for labour time. The market for wages is called the labour market and the price of wages, or wage levels, is determined to some extent by the supply and demand for labour. This is familiar territory for price theory. To take the example further, constant capital can be considered concretely as the cost of machinery, or capital goods to use the language of the mainstream, used in the production process. Interest and profit are returns to capital taken from the sale price of the product, or commodity, whose prices are determined by supply and demand in markets for capital goods. When grappling with Marx's rent theory, capital refers to value and revenues refer to price. This separation of categories and their systems of accounting is especially important when it comes to the notion of AR, its level being obtained by the difference between the value and price of commodities produced in the agricultural sector of capitalist economies.

The fact that land is privately owned in capitalism – governments can own land too and this is usually called public land but there is still a landowner – means that whoever owns the land must be paid for allowing access to it for production. This payment is called ground rent in Marx's schema. We saw earlier that the component of this payment that derived from the differing fertility of the land is called DR1, that which owed to the differing investments of capital on land are called DR2 and, finally, the amount paid for access to new lands irrespective of DR1 and DR2 is called AR. Capitalists cannot simply start investing in agricultural production. If Elon Musk suddenly decided that producing potatoes crossbred with marijuana was a good idea, he would still need to pay a landowner for access to the land to plant his new 'baked potatoes'. Sure, Musk might just decide to buy the land outright rather than lease it, but the price of the land would simply be the aggregate of rental fees over the number of years the landowner would have expected returns. Either way, Musk pays rent for access to land. This cost must figure into the price of the commodity produced for sale. If Elon decides to open 'baked potato' farms in what is currently the Yosemite National Park, pending the transfer of ownership from the federal to state governments,[40] Tesla may well be required to pay AR to the Treasury of California. If, however, Musk opts to rent or buy tracts of vineyards in the Napa Valley instead, the current owners of this land would be paid the equivalent amount of AR as DR2 for the reasons outlined above. Either way, the contours and rhythms of 'baked potato' production, alongside the fortunes of Tesla and capitalism in the United States, are affected by ground rent and capitalist landed property.

Marx's theory of rent is specific to land and to capitalism. Many argue that the theory dealt with feudal categories and is therefore redundant for analyses of modern capitalist societies, but this view is based on misunderstanding, or not having read, what Marx had to say on rent in various places across his enormous body of work. As one guide to *Capital* notes, Marx's theory of rent is 'probably the most complex application of his understanding of the capitalist economy'.[41] Its specificity means that so long as capitalism prevails and land is required in its social reproduction, Marx's theory of rent can illuminate the ways in which private ownership of land affects how society develops.

The next chapter introduces the mainstream approaches to rent theory that emerged not long after Marx's critique of the classical political economy. Whereas Marx's rent theory sought to tether rent to landed property in capitalism, the neoclassicals sever this connection by shifting their analysis of the economy to the sphere of exchange and thereby generalizing rents across all factors of production.

3
Mainstream Rent Theory

This chapter examines merits and limitations of mainstream rent theory. A few necessary but short preliminaries on what constitutes the mainstream approach to rent are followed by a brief look at definitions of rent from both popular and specialist sources. Short outlines of the various categories of rent that exist in the orthodox tradition are elaborated using examples to demonstrate the applicability of this mode of inquiry for practical purposes. Reflections on the core elements of mainstream rent theory conclude the discussion, providing points of departure for exploring alternatives offered up by modern political economy.

Debates about rent theory tend to reflect broader debates in economics. The questions posed by those seeking to clarify aspects of economic theory to do with rent ask questions like what is rent? How can rent be measured? Is rent important for explaining social problems and why? These types of questions coincide with others to do with economic theory more broadly, like what is value? What are the consequences for the distribution of value? What processes are responsible for creating value and is it ethical, moral and desirable to have value produced and allocated in specific ways?

The toolkits drawn upon to answer these questions can be considered different systems of knowledge, each with its own view of how the world works and, most importantly, each with a view of how the world should work. This point, about the normative dimension of all economic theory, is one of the key points of distinction splitting mainstream economics from political economy. The prevailing view in mainstream economics insists that an objective, value-free economic science is possible and that it is precisely what practitioners in the field should strive for. The point of reference for this approach was famously given expression by British economist Lionel Robbins who defined economics as 'the science which studies human behaviour as a relationship between ends and scarce means which have alternative uses'.[1] This relationship between scarce means with alternative uses and ends is particularly important for how the mainstream understands rent.

How exactly the economics vis-à-vis political economy terrain is defined is itself a contentious issue. There are those who make compelling arguments about the need to update and refine the critiques of so-called mainstream economics, claiming that the criticisms of an orthodoxy incapable of reconciling its ambitions for a scientific approach to economics with the subject matter of complex human societies is outdated or was perhaps misinformed to begin with.[2]

There are also good reasons to believe that one approach, usually referred to as neoclassical, remains the dominant methodological framework today when it comes to the teaching, practice and mode of economic inquiry. Irrespective of how many practitioners of economics consider themselves to be 'neoclassicals', the lexicon of economics today is governed by neoclassical principles, concepts and even avenues of inquiry. Or, to put this another way, the history of mainstream economics is bound up in the history of neoclassical thought because, while there is diversity in the mainstream today – behavioural economics, game theory, social choice theory, neuroeconomics, agent-based complexity theory and new institutional economics are held up as evidence that the 'neoclassical orthodoxy' no longer sets the research agenda in a much more pluralist mainstream in economics[3] – there is also continuity, in the reproduction of key conceptual apparatus, which constrains the capacity for deviation from the long-held propositions of neoclassicism.[4] Some claim that attempts to diversify the programme of research in a more pluralist mainstream have resulted in a reconfiguration, rather than rejection, of neoclassicism.[5] It is therefore reasonable to deem the neoclassical notion of rent as the mainstream approach to rent theory vis-à-vis alternative traditions of economic thought in general and to rent theory in particular. A cursory survey of definitions of rent found in economics dictionaries published in the twenty-first century gives an indication of how this orthodox view is articulated.

In its 'Economics A–Z', *The Economist* magazine provides the following definition for rent: 'confusingly, rent has two meanings for economists', the first, which is 'the commonplace definition', considers rent to be an 'income from hiring out land or other durable goods', whereas 'the second, also known as economic rent, is a measure of market power: the difference between what a factor of production is paid and how much it would need to be paid to remain in its current use.'[6] Market power in this context is when a buyer or seller in the market can exert significant influence over the quantity of goods and services traded or their sale price. The distorting influence of market power ceases to exist when there is perfect competition, but arises when there is a monopoly, monopsony or oligopoly. Income in this schema is 'the flow of money to the factors of production: wages to labour; profit to enterprise and capital; interest also to capital; rent to land'.[7]

Moving from the accessible and popular to the more specialized reference guides, *The New Palgrave Dictionary of Economics* defines rent as 'the payment for the use of a resource, whether it be land, labour, equipment, ideas, or even money' and 'economic rent' is payment for use of any resource whose supply is fixed.[8] Along similar lines, *The Routledge Dictionary of Economics* states rent is 'the charge imposed by the owner of property on another person wishing to use it' and this charge, called a rental payment, is payment for the use of a factor of production, while economic rent is part of the earnings of a factor owing to its scarcity.[9] While using slightly different ways to explain the concept, each of these definitions of rent emphasizes scarcity and the role of markets in determining the level of rental payment. Below are some of the particular forms of rent that can be obtained within this framework of knowledge.

Economic rent

The descriptor 'economic' was added to the word 'rent' by neoclassical economists in the nineteenth century who claimed that what they once thought applied to land alone was in fact more common. Land was considered to be in finite supply because humans could not produce more of it. This absolute scarcity meant that no amount of money could bring more of it into existence. This was considered not to be the case with people or with machinery. Populations could be deliberately increased if the needs of those extra people were provided for. Machines could be manufactured faster or in larger quantities so long as the means to produce them were in abundance alongside enough people to work them up into usable goods. But it soon became clear to neoclassical economists that people too were scarce when food crops failed or when war and pestilence killed them. Machinery might also be considered scarce at times when coal was hard to come by for keeping furnaces alight or when skilled labour was hard to find. The economic form of rent was therefore conceived to account for the way scarcity affected the price of all forms of property used in production and not just land.

Economic rent is the amount paid for a factor of production over and above what is necessary to keep that factor in its current use. Factors of production are land, labour and capital. Some economists believe that capital can be split into two, creating a fourth factor of production, entrepreneurship. Each factor receives income in return for its use in the production process. These factor incomes are wages for labour, rent for land, interest for capital and profit for entrepreneurship. In the simplified three-factor model of land, labour and capital, the income for capital can be both interest and profit. The expanded model would claim that interest is the income for capital and profit the income for entrepreneurship. Note, too, that rent as the factor income for the owner of land is technically distinct from the economic rent of land. A landowner might well receive rent from a tenant, but some of that rental payment might be considered economic rent in excess of the minimum payment for land because they have more fertile soil than their neighbour or a more attractive view. More on this later. Payment in this context is monetary and the amount required to keep a factor in its present use is called its opportunity cost. The word 'use' refers to employment, and the factors of production are purchased in markets for labour, land and capital.

Rent considered in this context is legible only with basic familiarity of the terminology of neoclassical economics. Like any language, this terminology evolved in a specific historical context. This context is significant because it encompasses the immediate past, and therefore has conditioned the present state of things, in mainstream rent theory.

Money, markets and modernity are the invisible foundations upon which the concept of economic rent is built. If any of these elements were missing – a modern monetary system, markets through which most are compelled to interact in order to subsist, a global capitalist system where most people rely on waged labour to live – the concept of economic rent could not exist. This form of rent is the most recent substantive development in a long line of historical changes to the relationships between people that constitute the rental payment for the use of property.

Before moving on to some examples to flesh out these rather abstract concerns, it is worth noting that just because this form of rent is considered to be the latest iteration, that does not mean it is the only form of rent that currently exists. Alaskan oil royalties, for example, can still be paid 'in kind' if the state so chooses.[10] This simply means that if the Alaskan state government decides one year that they need oil rather than money, they can insist that oil companies to whom they have granted rights to drill oil, or leases, must pay their rent in kind, as barrels of oil, rather than in money. This is perhaps only a superficial distinction between monetary forms of rent and rent in kind because the price of the oil is still regulated by the interactions of market mechanisms embedded within monetary economies. The significance of this will be discussed further in chapter 4 but the point to note for now is that the historical forms of rent can and do co-exist with the current prevailing form, of monetary rent, but it is the dominant form of rent that sets the conditions for the others to arise. Now for some further examples of economic rent that demonstrate how it arises with respect to each factor of production.

The old adage that one would not get out of bed for less than such and such amount of money is one example of economic rent. The supermodel Linda Evangelista once told a reporter in October 1990 that 'we have this saying, Christy [Turlington] and I . . . we don't wake up for less than $10,000 a day.'[11] If Evangelista and Turlington were offered $15,000 for a day's work, the economic rent they would receive is $5,000. This is because, by their own admission, the amount necessary to keep the factor of production they own in use, their labour, is but a mere $10,000 per day. The total factor income, what they get paid in return for their contribution to the production process, is therefore comprised of two elements in this case. On the one hand, they receive the market price of their labour, which is the $10,000 minimum they themselves set, as the factor income for labour, known as wages. On the other hand, they receive the economic rent of labour, which could be referred to as a labour rent, as the excess above the market price of their labour. While Evangelista's accountant might consider the entire $15,000 payment as 'wages' when lodging a tax return, a labour market economist analysing wage growth in the fashion industry would be more discerning, splitting the total income into $10,000 of wages and $5,000 of economic rent. They receive this rent because, as supermodels, they are perceived to own a rare form of labour, one that only certain individuals can perform. Moreover, the capacity to perform this labour is not something that can be taught or trained – i.e., produced. The labourer must be born with whatever it is that designers and purveyors of haute couture covet at the time. Their labour is therefore scarce and not able to be produced, making its supply inelastic relative to its price.

Continuing on in the epistemic universe, or framework of knowledge, of neoclassical economics, the economic rent of capital appears as what are sometimes called 'super profits'. These are above-average profits that exceed the cost of production plus the opportunity cost of the total capital invested. Capital in this context does not mean money. Rather, capital refers to the things that money can buy, which are not land and labour or the raw materials used in production, but that produce commodities. A sewing machine purchased for use in the home would not be considered capital, for example. But if the owner of the machine starts using it to embroider old shirts and sells them at the local artisan market, the machine becomes capital. The key point is that capital is something used to produce commodities for sale that is not land, labour or raw materials. The opportunity cost of capital is the normal profit that could be expected to be earned in another industry with a similar degree of risk involved.

Examples of the economic rent of capital include the extra profit that Apple and Samsung receive relative to competitors like Huawei, owing to patents on things like battery technology that ensure superior performance for their smartphones. In the final quarter of 2020, Apple shipped almost 80 million phones, while Samsung managed 62 million only, almost doubling Huawei's 34 million.[12] It might well be difficult to determine how many phones were sold because of ownership of specific capital goods, like iPhone battery technology, but whatever the share of total profits for Apple derived solely from owning such technologies, this would be considered economic rent.

The economic rent of land appears as the excess profits that derive from the degree of competition, or lack thereof, in the market for land. Land does not necessarily just mean a chunk of space but also its appurtenances, such as soil fertility, mineral deposits or even location. If the unique quality of some piece of land enters into the production process of some good or service which then sells at a higher price than those of competitor firms, the amount of the price left over after costs of production and the opportunity cost of capital, or average profit, in another industry with a similar degree of risk, is called the economic rent of land. Countries that have an abundance of oil reserves, for example, are said to be the beneficiaries of economic rents that arise from their sale of oil. Companies drilling oil in places like Nigeria and Australia gain access to what is called sweet crude, which has a sulphur content below 0.5%, whereas those extracting oil in the Gulf of Mexico or Alaska find sour crude, which has a sulphur content above 0.5%. Sweet crude is preferred by most refiners because it has fewer impurities and is therefore less costly to refine.[13] This preference is reflected in the pricing of crude oil, with companies selling sweet crude fetching higher prices than those selling equivalent amounts of sour crude. If the worst sour crude price sets the lowest possible profit for crude oil, then any excess in price above this benchmark would be considered economic rent.

The distinction between rent and economic rent is most apparent when it comes to land because the two forms exist side by side. A rent is paid by the tenant to the landowner for the use of the land, but the economic rent exists separately. The way to make sense of the difference is competition. To continue with the oil example above, sour crude oil is the worst quality due to its level of impurities, making it more costly to refine. The market price of crude, its minimum opportunity cost, or the very least amount of profit someone looking to get into oil production could make, is the price of sour crude. The sour stuff costs more to refine so profits from the sale of the finished product are eroded by the high cost of production. Sour crude is therefore the least popular form of crude. When it comes to all the potential oil leases for sale, sour crude leases in Alaska are cheaper than the very lucrative sweet crude leases in Nigeria. We can then say that when it comes to the payment for land for the purposes of producing oil, the level of that payment, the rent, is set by the marginal, or worst, lands.

But not everyone can afford to buy Alaskan oil leases. Anyone in the oil business, however, could readily buy Alaskan leases, whereas the purchase of Nigerian sweet crude leases would be more difficult because they are more sought after. Economic rent, in this context, can therefore be measured as any deviation from the price of the Alaskan leases. But this would be the case only if all owners of lands with oil knew only of the reserves of sour crude and auctioned off all their leases at the same time. The companies that did the drilling would then all make different profits on the basis of the differing qualities of crude or indeed because some companies could afford to buy longer drills or more efficient pumps. This would not last, though, because as soon as the leases ended, the landowners would realize that their land was generating extra profits for the oil company owing to the sweetness of their crude. When it came time to renegotiating the next lease agreement, the landowner would increase the rent to precisely the point at which the oil company could still make the same profit as the sour crude leases produced for their companies because that is the minimum profit an oil company in this hypothetical example can make.

To summarize, according to the neoclassical view, economic rent is the component of price paid to the owner of a factor of production in excess of the amount necessary to maintain that factor in its current use. The reason this economic rent exists, or why someone would pay more than what was necessary to bring that factor into use, is because the supply of that factor is fixed. This scarcity or exclusivity means that as demand rises, competition for the purchase and use of that factor is increased but supply remains constant, bidding up its price and therefore generating economic rent. Land was initially considered the only factor of production that had fixed supply. The adjective 'economic' was supposedly added to rent to indicate that there were other factors of production that could also be considered as having fixed supply relative to demand.[14] Whether or not this fixity of supply is temporary or permanent was the specific problem that led to the development of the theory of quasi-rent, to be elaborated in the next section.

Non-economic rent, or simply, rent, is a more generic term that describes the income received by the owner of property, with a supply that is not fixed, and is therefore sensitive to price, for permitting its use. Scooters and houses are to non-economic rent what supermodel labour, Nigerian oil leases and iPhone batteries are to economic rent for the mainstream.

The key characteristic of rent in the neoclassical view is the relationship between scarcity and time. Scarcity is less a description of the material abundance of a particular thing, but rather its scarcity in relation to demand in a given market. Coal, for example, is not actually scarce. The 2015 Paris climate summit revealed that more than 80% of the proven coal reserves in the world would need to remain buried if the climate change mitigation targets set at that conference were to be reached.[15] The alternative, presumably, is that digging up this coal and burning it would mean an end to life on earth brought about by catastrophic global warming. In which case, there would be nobody around to use coal as a factor of production. In this sense, coal is the opposite of scarce. However, in relation to the demand for coal in current industrial processes, there is a relative scarcity.

The absolute scarcity of land means that its capacity for generating rent, a payment for a factor in excess of its opportunity cost, is permanent. This is why, according to the neoclassical view, rent was initially considered a factor income specific to land. When it became clear that other factors could also be considered scarce in the context of the neoclassical conceptualization of the economy, labour and capital were also brought into the theory of economic rent. There is more to the story of how the neoclassical view of rent came to pass. This is discussed later. Suffice it to say for now that prices obtained through the simultaneous interactions of supply and demand in the markets for factors of production, which is the basis of general equilibrium in the neoclassical framework, has logical consequences for the theory of rent that is possible in neoclassical economics.

Quasi-rent

Quasi-rent refers to a form of economic rent that disappears over time. The scarcity of the factor of production in question, relative to its demand, is not permanent but, rather, short-lived. For the duration of this period of fixed supply, or scarcity relative to demand, the asset or factor is considered to generate a quasi-rent. Quasi simply means almost, which denotes that this short-lived economic rent is almost an economic rent, but not quite.

The experience of the Covid-19 pandemic is replete with examples of quasi-rents because, it is hoped, there might be some future point in time where the conditions of the pandemic no longer prevail, meaning that the scarcity of certain factors of production will be eroded away by changes in their supply and the demand for them. The capital, labour and land involved in the production of face masks and personal protective equipment, for example, are all currently earning quasi-rents for their owners because the temporary conditions for increased demand currently prevail. Once the pandemic ends, however, the demand for face masks and personal protective equipment will, presumably, decrease and a corresponding change in price will occur, calling into production less capital, labour and land for future rounds of production, eroding quasi-rents.

The original sense in which quasi-rent was used referred to the temporary period in which the supply for capital goods – goods that are used in the production of other goods – was insensitive to price. In this context, almost all capital goods generate a quasi-rent for at least a short period of time. Consider, for example, the purchase of a commercial bread oven to realize the dream of opening an artisan bakery after spending the Covid-19 pandemic in lockdown perfecting sourdough baking techniques. With each round of production of these niche ovens, the supply is fixed relative to demand for as long as it takes to produce the next round. Therefore, while all prospective artisan bakers have purchased ovens and the next lot are in the process of being made, the oven makers and the people they purchase inputs from are paid a quasi-rent because their product is relatively scarce for a discrete period of time.

Monopoly rent

Monopoly rent refers to the component of price paid to the owner of a factor of production that derives specifically from their monopoly position in a corresponding market. Lance Armstrong, for example, was once considered to have a monopoly on the freakish ability to keep winning the Tour de France. The monopoly rent gained from Armstrong's unique cycling ability netted him a personal worth of around US$125 million at the height of his career in 2012.[16] This form of economic rent is directly determined by the degree of competition in a given market. Monopoly technically refers to a market dominated by a single seller, but it need not always, indicating in a more general sense the distortion of competition through collusion and other actions concentrating power over market processes.[17] The total absence of competition, or movement towards it, therefore means that monopoly producers can charge what they like for their products, with limitations being placed only by the capacity for potential buyers to spend.

Monopolies come about by coincidence or design. Natural monopolies, for example, occur in industries where there are very high costs associated with production, presenting barriers to entry that are simply insurmountable for most firms. The space exploration and travel industry might be considered ripe for monopoly when the infrastructural costs associated with building, maintaining and operating space-craft are considered. Similarly, telecommunications and the provision of other utilities like electricity and water have typically been considered natural monopolies owing to the high cost of infrastructural set-up and also because competition in the delivery of these services may not be efficient. Imagine a situation where there were several firms all digging up the pavement in a suburban street because they all needed to lay their own fibre optic cables in order to deliver internet services to the houses in the street that subscribed to their services. This happened in Italy in 2017, where firms competing to provide internet services to the good people of Perugia found themselves digging trenches side by side on cramped streets to ensure competition kept prices down for consumers.[18] That the firms ended up blowing their infra-structure budgets and passing on the costs to those same consumers might prompt cause for reflection on why natural monopolies are so called.

Aside from natural monopolies, the manipulation of competition in markets can be coordinated by economic actors themselves, generating opportunities for monopoly rent. Firms can coordinate supply, for example, directly stifling competition and thereby manipulating prices. This is commonly referred to as cartel behaviour and there are rather infamous examples, both historically and more recently. The Kimberley Process Certification System that began in 2003 sought to mitigate the capacity for diamond producers to appropriate monopoly rents through their manipulation of diamond supplies which fuelled trade in blood diamonds, for example. Similarly, consumers can band together to coordinate their consumption choices to manipulate demand and therefore directly impact the level of monopoly rents that producers can access. The obverse of monopoly is monopsony, where a market is characterized by a single buyer. In the case of ethical consumerism, the power of monopsony is used to sanction monopoly producers. Ethical consumption initiatives like the boycotting of fashion brands for the use of exploitative labour practices in their supply chains is one example. The 'Heart Foundation Tick' campaign, launched by McDonald's in response to the film *Supersize Me*, is also evidence of the capacity for consumers to affect demand and to therefore erode the capacity for firms to appropriate monopoly rents. Finally, the state, or government, as the rule-makers for markets, can also affect the degree of competition in markets for factors of production through various measures. The lockdowns in response to the Covid-19 pandemic are a case in point, where governments around the world made choices about which firms could operate, effectively determining the degree of competition and also, therefore, the potential for firms to extract monopoly rents. Finally, to return to the Armstrong example above, it turned out that what people thought was a natural monopoly arising from freakish talent was in fact confected through hard work and the consistent use of performance-enhancing drugs. The level of monopoly rent in this case is indicated by Armstrong's admission that once his doping regime was discovered, he lost at least US$75 million in endorsements and legal fees.[19]

Economic rents indicate a degree of competition in markets for factors of production. Quasi-rents and monopoly rents are specific forms of economic rent. Quasi-rent is a function of temporality, or of a discrete and short time period for the economic rent to exist. Competition is constrained in this sense because of time. Monopoly rent, however, refers more to the fact that competition is constrained due to the lack of sellers in the markets for factors of production.

Rent seeking

The capacity for the state to create the conditions for the extraction of monopoly rents relates specifically to the notion of rent seeking. Firms lobbying the state to enact laws or to implement regimes of regulation that manipulate the degree of competition in markets where they operate are considered to be engaging in rent-seeking behaviour. This concept was popularized in pioneering studies of rent seeking by Anne Krueger in 1974 and Gordon Tullock in 1967. Krueger's study looked at the ways in which import licences and quantitative restrictions on imports led to increasing lobbying from the private sector of government to gain favourable conditions in a bid to bolster their market power.[20] Tullock's study of monopoly and theft argued that welfare economics had not accounted for the cost of firms seeking to establish monopoly and its benefits when taking account of the overall cost of monopolizing behaviour. This finding pointed out that firms would aspire to monopoly because they could see the potential for its benefits even if they were not assured of success. Therefore, if the overall cost of monopoly to the economy was to be considered, the failures needed to be counted along with the successes because firms would all try, even if most failed.[21] The concept of rent seeking emerged in the context of a broader assault on the role of the state, wherein its efficiency was questioned in view of corruption.[22]

This line of inquiry has been fertile ground for those looking at the relationships between economic dynamism, the appropriate role of the state in the economy and, in particular, the effects of rent seeking on economic development. Some recent studies highlight the capacity for 'rent seeking' to influence economic development in low- and middle-income countries. One such study by Ahmed on rentier capitalism in Pakistan suggests the following characterization, whereby rent seeking is 'capturing, in whole or in part, the value addition of others', which includes but is not limited to 'influence peddling, deal-making, acquiring access to scarce assets on the basis of connections'.[23] Others consider 'neo-patrimonialism' in Africa wherein growth 'is constrained by a governance system in which national leaders or "big men" secure their legitimacy by allocating lucrative but unproductive economic opportunities to their clients or cronies'.[24] Indeed, Kelsall goes on to say that 'political clientelism is an inevitable feature of all developing countries and rent-seeking exists wherever there are imperfect markets.'[25] More sophisticated analyses question the usual association between democratic institutions and the capacity for

rent-seeking behaviour to proliferate, favouring an approach
that acknowledges the different structural factors present
in low-income countries such as large informal
significant non-market accumulation and the use
to create rents to benefit factions in power.[26]

The logic of the argument that underpins the
concept is fairly intuitive. Firms, or economi
subject to forces of competition and therefore se
some degree of control over those forces by in
energy and resources into campaigns to lol
apparatus to provide favourable treatment thro
and legislative channels. The least sophisticat
this argument might draw associations betwee
weakness of political institutions in poorer par
and the capacity for vested interests to take a
perceived weakness to increase their share of
More nuanced arguments might call into foc
nature of political and economic institution
across the spectrum of national income leve
for the structural components of rent-seeki
be explored.

This concludes the discussion of mainstream rent theory.
Figure 3.1 below provides a point of reference for the
discussion of key forms of rent that constitute the mainstream
approach.

The relationship between scarcity and time, in the context
of markets for factors of production, was emphasized to
understand the various rent categories that cascade from
the generalization of perceived properties of land across to
labour and capital. Rent in this view is always associated
with monopoly but not necessarily with land. The merits of
this approach are that rent helps explain the consequences
of monopoly in the ownership of factors of production.
Moreover, the role of competition in facilitating or mitigating
the formation of monopoly, and therefore rents, is clear.
Solutions to the problem of rents are therefore relatively
easily conceived, albeit much harder to implement effectively.
Rents are a sign of poorly performing markets and therefore
states should intervene to fix them. The limitations of the
approach might be that rent depends upon stylized conceptions of markets and the actors that constitute them. Further

Figure 3.1 Orthodox (neoclassical) rent theory

Type of rent	Brief definition	Source of rent	Examples
Economic rent	The amount paid to an owner of a factor of production over and above what is necessary to keep that factor in its current use	Scarcity and/or exclusivity	Payments for highly skilled labour such as that exhibited by elite athletes and artists.
(Non-economic) rent	Income received by the owner of property for permitting its use	Property rights, ownership and control	Housing rent, Netflix fee, train, bus or taxi fare
Quasi-rent	Economic rent that is timebound	Scarcity and time	The amount of inflation in the price of hand sanitizer since the start of the covid-19 pandemic till its end
Monopoly rent	In a market dominated by a single seller (i.e., a monopoly) the owner of the factor would receive economic rent in the form of monopoly rent	Concentrated market power resulting in the absence of competition	The price of a ticket on Elon Musk's space bus
Rent seeking	Firm behaviour that seeks to influence governments to intervene in the operation of free markets to stifle competition to their benefit	Unnecessary government intervention in the operation of the economy for the purpose of personal gain (i.e., corruption)	Corporate lobby groups
Scarcity rent	An earlier form of economic rent used to describe the difference between the cost of a factor of production and the price of output from its use which derived not from differing quality of the factor itself but from the absolute scarcity of that factor	Absolute scarcity and scarcity relative to demand	The price of corn produced by large agribusiness firms with economies of scale relative to smallholdings and family farms
Resource rent	The economic rent paid to owners of natural resources	The material characteristics of land and its bounty mediated through property rights	Fees to enter national parks

limitations are spotlighted in the next chapter on the political economy critique of mainstream rent theory.

Neoclassicals and the 'end of history' for rent?

Mainstream economics enjoyed what some have dubbed a 'formalist revolution' from the 1950s. This was a period in which the conceptual apparatus of neoclassical economics became highly mathematical. The formalist takeover during the 1950s was marked by the publication in 1954 of a paper by Kenneth Arrow and Gerard Debreu asserting a mathematical proof of Walrasian general equilibrium theory.[27] These two would later receive the Sveriges Riksbank Prize in Memory of Alfred Nobel for the Economic Sciences (the so-called Nobel Prize in Economics). The article is still regarded to this day as rigorous proof of general equilibrium in a market economy that fulfilled the dream of Léon Walras, a nineteenth-century French economist who pioneered theories of market equilibrium.[28] The Arrow–Debreu proof was praised for its innovative use of new mathematical techniques, such as the replacement of differential calculus with convex analysis, the use of relatively new instruments like Nash equilibria and game theory, and the characterization of equilibria by separation theorems rather than tangencies.[29]

Arrow and Debreu's 1954 article is also considered one of the earliest dramatic uses in economics of the 'indirect, non-constructive proof method' of modern mathematics, whereby Brouwer's 'fixed-point theorem' is used to prove the existence of general equilibrium through logical implication by virtue of its axioms rather than by any reference to material reality.[30] The Arrow–Debreu proof took the economic problem of the possibility of simultaneous market equilibrium in a real economy and turned it into a mathematical problem about a virtual economy, which would be held to the standards of abstract mathematics rather than empirical economics.[31] The burden of proof was rigorous and logical but the link to material reality had been severed in favour of logical consistency and axiomatic causation. Such developments in the techniques of economic theorizing have been appropriately labelled 'formalism run riot'.[32] Arrow and Debreu were pioneers of modern economic methods by virtue of uniting the threads of general equilibrium theory and mathematical formalism. This unity of marginalist principles and formalist methods is typical of the orthodoxy in rent theory today.

The significance of the Arrow–Debreu proof for the theorization of rent is twofold. First, this formalist proof of general equilibrium theory settled an argument carried on within marginalist economics since the turn of the century. On the one hand were supporters of Walras and William Stanley Jevons, who applied the principles of marginalism within the context of general equilibrium, in opposition to those adherents of Alfred Marshall, who worked within a framework of partial equilibrium.[33] Second, by the high-water mark of the formalist period, the Arrow–Debreu proof signalled the 'end of history' for the methodology of orthodox economics. The technical apparatus and technical architecture of the economic sciences from this point on was apparently settled in favour of a unity between marginalist principles and formalist method. The theory of rent corresponding to this epistemological and ontological framework has been effectively uncontested within the orthodoxy to the present day.

The orthodox theory of rent does not entail a theory of property that is specific to the society in which rents are generated and distributed. This point can be taken further when it is considered alongside the technical aspects of marginalist rent theory. The first question to be asked is: does a theory of rent need to be distinguishable from a theory of profit or wages? Rent in the classical schema was the factor income derived from the ownership of land. This distinction becomes a casualty of the marginalist revolution from the 1870s. Whether it be within the framework of general or partial equilibrium, rent cannot be distinguished from profits or wages because factor incomes are determined by factor prices. In the general equilibrium model, all factor prices are determined simultaneously, and rent is therefore a derivative of prices affected by supply and demand in each market. In the partial equilibrium model, the rest of the economy must be exogenously fixed and a one-good world assumed. This type of analysis must also be based on the assumption of a fixed and indestructible supply of land. In both cases, the specificity of rent as a distinct revenue is logically denied.[34] The consequences of this framing of rent are taken up in the next chapter which surveys political economy alternatives to rent theory.

4
Rent Theory in Modern Political Economy

The study of economics is political. Modern political economy begins from this principle, providing a contrast to mainstream economics by spotlighting the inherently political character of economic phenomena, contrary to the claims of mainstream economists pursuing apparently value-free lines of inquiry.[1] The descriptor, 'modern', simply distinguishes political economy today from classical political economy, which is what preceded the discipline of economics. To understand the motivations behind this rebranding exercise, one need only ask why Alfred Marshall's 1890 *Principles of Economics* deliberately dropped what John Stuart Mill had seen fit to include in his 1848 *Principles of Political Economy*.

What exactly constitutes this 'contrast' to economics and what does this mean for rent theory? A few key points of difference with respect to methodology are important for understanding political economy approaches to rent, otherwise known as heterodox rent theory.

First, political economists take issue with three 'separations' that inform the mainstream: the separation of economics from politics; the separation of economic theory from socio-economic reality; and the separation of economics from ecology.[2] The latter two separations are arguably one and the same because the material basis of the socio-economic reality is the ecology in which it is inextricably embedded, although the explicit emphasis on ecological concerns is worth prioritizing in a critique of the mainstream.

The first separation is of direct consequence for mainstream rent theory, particularly in relation to the rent-seeking literature. The core question underlying the rent-seeking concept regards the appropriate role of the state in the economy? What appears as a perfectly sensible and indeed commonly asked question has embedded within it the scope of possible answers. The state is conceived as external to the economy so therefore any response must necessarily accept this frame of reference. The state is always seen as intervening in the operation of an economic system that would otherwise function according to its own self-regulating laws of motion. This is not to deny that useful insights can be derived from such a perspective, but the point to note is that this separation of the political and the economic, of the economy and of the state, constrains potential solutions because of the way the problem has been constructed. It is no wonder that scholars like Mushtaq Khan, who advocates for placing more emphasis on the structural aspects of low-income countries rather than relying on generic characterizations of rent-seeking behaviour and state corruption, are critical outliers in the rent-seeking scholarship.

Mainstream economics is also considered by political economists to hinge on three problematic core principles: (1) methodological individualism: denies structural analysis except when individual behaviour is aggregated; (2) methodological instrumentalism: behaviour is preference driven and means–end focused; (3) theory is equilibrium directed: mathematics in the mainstream assumes existence of equilibria, assumes how it can be found and assumes that no forces exist to permanently deny equilibria, misrepresenting reality.[3] The scaffold for this methodology has been described as TA x TA, where a 'technical apparatus', utility functions and production functions are deployed through a 'technical architecture', consisting of three fundamental tenets of the optimizing behaviour of individuals and firms, of the scarcity postulate and of general equilibrium.[4] The survey of mainstream rent theory in the previous chapter demonstrated the application of this methodology to questions of rent.

The political economy critique of mainstream rent theory is made up of diverse viewpoints, united perhaps only by the fact they are critical of these foundational elements of the neoclassical approach. Some common lines of criticism have emerged. Individual agency is clearly an element in the determination of rents but so too is the social structure to which individuals belong. Behaviour is conditioned by preferences but in the context of changing circumstances, particularly when it comes to situations when rents arise. Equilibrium in markets is merely another state that requires explanation, as are monopoly situations, rather than the norm. These criticisms are just a few of the insights that heterodox approaches to rent theory assert.

The following sections will elaborate in brief some of these threads. It is tempting to label each contribution as belonging to a school of thought or some kind of tradition in economic theory but to do so might obfuscate the real story of rent: how it is that a revenue specifically related to land comes to be applied to all factors of production and to what end. It is worth bearing in mind the earlier discussion of the two broad orientations in rent theory, emphasizing land or monopoly. The first contribution to the political economy critique of the mainstream takes up both land and monopoly in rent theory. Those that follow take up various themes such as feminist, ecological, institutionalist and policy-oriented critiques of mainstream rent theory.

World mining rent and financialized food

The critique of mainstream rent theory to come out of the historical materialist approach has tended to emphasize the role of private property in capitalism affecting social development. On the one hand, there are those who consider the role of rent theory is to explain how it is that the private ownership of the means to produce things in capitalism generates a specific type of revenue: rents. On the other hand, there are those who think that not only is the fact of private ownership of the means of production in capitalism important, but it is the very form which that ownership takes that is critical to understanding the role of rents in the development of capitalism. The former approach takes the view that rent does not necessarily apply to land only, whereas the latter considers a theory of rent to be contingent upon a theory of capitalist landed property.

Two examples of these approaches are the concept of world mining rents and the systems of provision approach applied to food. Both draw on historical materialist critiques of mainstream rent theory, but they do so through differing interpretations of the theory of rent that has evolved in historical materialist discourse since the 1860s. This line of inquiry differed from the prevailing theory of rent at that time by claiming that the source of rent was the system of landed property in capitalism rather than the land itself. This simply meant that while many saw the differing fertility of land as the source of rents – land next to rivers meant better crop yields, for example – historical materialists claimed that it was rather the fact that someone could own that land and determine the conditions of its use (control) in the context of capitalist industry that generated rent. This insight represented an important break from the prevailing view of rent, and it is on this basis that others have extended historical materialist rent theory. Let us now look at what these applications of historical materialist rent theory can tell us about rent today and, more importantly, how they offer alternatives to the mainstream theory of rent examined earlier.

The first example is world mining rents. This concept was pioneered by Chibuzo Nnate Nwoke in the 1980s in studies of Nigerian political economy within the context of the capitalist world system. Nwoke saw that while countries like Nigeria had an abundance of oil, they seemed unable to reap the benefits of that natural resource endowment. Nwoke took historical materialist concepts, based on Marx's rent theory, and applied them to the global minerals industry to make sense of why this might be the case. To summarize Nwoke in very basic terms, historical materialist rent theory claimed that there were three types of rent. There were two types of differential rent and one type of absolute rent. Differential rent was the payment for the use of land above the least fertile land that was owed to either the natural fertility of the land or to the different levels of capital applied to the land. For example, if Nigerian sweet crude fetched more than Alaskan sour crude in oil markets, the difference between them would be considered a differential rent type 1. If two oil leases of equal size and with equal quality oil in Alaska made different profits over the same period, then it was probably due to one having a more productive drill. This difference in revenue derived from a differential rent type 2. The final category of rent was called absolute rent, and this was owed to the fact that oil leases all over the world were able to be owned at all and from the types of ownership through which they were made accessible. If all oil-lease owners in the world decided, for example, to stop people accessing their land, oil prices would go through the roof and the subsequent revenues might be considered absolute rent.

Nwoke argued that in the early 1980s, the world mining industry was characterized by resource-rich nation-states acting as landowners, while multinational mining companies were the tenant miners. In this view, the governments of host countries should be able to appropriate mineral rents by virtue of their ownership of the minerals in the ground. Unfortunately, from Nwoke's perspective, the multinational companies were able to misappropriate these rents for a few reasons. First, the nature of mining at the time meant that operations were very large scale and were therefore dependent on expensive machinery and the associated technology and skillsets to put them to work. This meant that even if the host governments technically could deny the companies leases to their mineral lands, the companies could seek out other sources of minerals while withholding the machinery, skilled labour and technology necessary for extracting the minerals. This was how companies were able to misappropriate differential rents 1 and 2. When it came to absolute rent, host governments were unable to capitalize on these at all because the need for mining investment was so great amongst the resource-rich but capital-poor countries of the global South that they were willing to undercut their neighbours to ensure they got a slice of the investment pie. It was these mechanisms, Nwoke argued, that kept mineral-rich countries poor. This was contrary to the mainstream theory of resource rents at the time which claimed that these countries should be able to assert their power as owners of minerals to generate higher profit margins through extracting their 'free gifts of nature' and then deploying these funds into developing other parts of their economies. By applying historical materialist notions of rent to modern mining, Nwoke was able to show that the owners of land were no longer able to hold onto the rents that their status as property owners once permitted.[5]

World mining rent considered in this way is a departure from the mainstream approach to rent because it explains how the owner of minerals does not necessarily receive the benefits of that ownership. However, although Nwoke's approach draws on historical materialist concepts, it still accepts, in part, that rent is really about monopoly. In this particular case, the emphasis is on minerals, which are drawn from land, but essentially the concern is about the ways in which multinational corporations are able to use their monopoly power to wrest away rent from host governments. An alternative view is to be found in the systems of provision approach to consumption theory. The following example of this approach being applied to food demonstrates what a historical materialist approach to rent theory, with an emphasis on landed property, can tell us.

The systems of provision (SoP) approach to consumption deploys a notion of rent that tethers it to land, or, more specifically, a theory of capitalist landed property. Rather than conceiving of production and consumption as applying horizontally across some or all sectors of the economy, the systems of provision approach consider them as vertically integrated through intermediate activities like design, distribution, retailing and preference formation through material culture.[6] This means that different commodity groups are produced and consumed through different systems of provision, drawing on distinctive forms and structures of these intermediate activities. It is not altogether difficult to imagine that the systems of producing, distributing, exchanging and consuming food, for example, might be markedly different than those involved in the same activities for clothing, energy or transport.

This perspective allows for the limitations of things like ethical consumption to be theorized in the context of changes in the structures of industries and the ways in which commodities are produced, distributed and consumed. The significance of this approach for rent theory is that the notion of rent articulated through the SoP approach rests on an understanding of rent that presupposes a connection to historically specific forms of landed property. That is, this view of rent is not oriented towards subordinating rent theory to a theory of monopoly. Rather, this view seeks to establish rent as a distinct revenue deriving from the historically specific forms of ownership and control of land. As such, the notion of rent in the SoP approach is not merely a distributional concern – i.e., concerned with the divvying up of the profits after produced goods are sold – but one that can affect patterns of capital accumulation – i.e., how production itself is organized. Importantly, rent enters into consideration in the SoP approach only insofar as it is the payment for the use of landed property.

To put it another way, most theories of rent consider it to be a revenue that is allocated after production occurs, meaning that any fluctuations in the level of rent or who it might go to does not impact how production is organized and carried out. A tax on mining activity, for example, which aims to appropriate rents for the government that controls access to the minerals on behalf of its citizenry, is supposed to be a neutral tax because it should not disincentivize investment in new mines. This is because economic rent, in the mainstream view, is the amount over and above the cost of production plus profit that could be achieved in another industry with similar risk. A billion-dollar investment in a new iron ore mine should not be put off by a new tax on economic rent of iron ore production because the return would be the same if that money was invested in steel making or the construction industry.

According to the SoP notion of rent, however, the rental payment is not merely something divvied up after production has occurred but rather rent has the capacity to affect the very organization of production. If the billionaire investor from before was not happy about the new tax, they may well decide to seek to realize the profit they stand to lose elsewhere, like in steel making or indeed in construction. They may well divest from the country where the mining tax was implemented altogether, choosing to bankroll a competing industry in another country to spite the government trying to tax the economic rent to which neoclassical rent theory claims they are entitled. Perhaps this is what was meant by Rio Tinto boss Tom Albanese when, at a 2010 dinner at Lord's Cricket

Ground in London, not ten days after the prime minister of Australia had been removed from office by his own party due to an unpopular mining tax, he warned that 'Policymakers around the world can learn a lesson when considering a new tax to plug a revenue gap, or play to local politics.'[7]

Technoscience rent

Technological rent is considered the part of monopoly profits created by the use of technical innovations to increase labour productivity.[8] Technical progress in this context is measured as changes in output as a consequence of a change in a particular production technique, the speed of production or by noticeable improvements in the quality of the product.[9] Monopoly profit refers to profits that are in excess of what is normal for a given market, owing to some advantage that a producer has that other producers in that market do not have access to. In the case of technology rent, the source of the super or monopoly profit is the ownership, to the exclusion of all others, of some kind of technology that gives that producer the ability to charge more for their product, thereby leading to excess profit above the industry average. The term 'technoscience rent' has been used recently to describe economic rents that derive from the technical-economic character of the asset that generates rents, as well as the juridical relationship, or property rights, which make it tradeable.[10]

Examples of this kind of rent can be found across several industries. Apple instigated a 'design patent war' with its rival Samsung in 2011 by filing claims in US courts alleging Samsung had infringed software patents relating to its iPhone.[11] The patent war was finally declared over in 2018 after a California court ordered Samsung to pay Apple US$539 million on top of an undisclosed out-of-court settlement.[12] At issue were several software and battery technologies that were considered the source of Apple's competitive advantage in the market for smartphones. The modern agriculture firm, Monsanto, has been patenting seed technology for several years, ensuring food production globally relies on paying them rents for access to seeds. This has been referred to by some as 'corporate rent seeking'[13] and by others as the use of intellectual property rights to secure monopoly profits.[14] Whatever the practice is called, the mechanism by which Monsanto uses its ownership of technology to secure payment for access to resources integral to food production is well-established practice in modern agriculture. These practices have been further entrenched by changes in the global regulatory frameworks enforced by organizations like the World Trade Organization and the International Monetary Fund.

While the literature on technoscience rent illuminates the ways in which new forms of assets can generate rents, the theory of rent itself remains a function of scarcity and is concerned primarily with monopoly. The contribution from this literature is to help make sense of how technology, innovation and science coalesce within the context of twenty-first-century capitalism to create new iterations of old forms of rent.

Land rent at the margins

Land rent is the payment for the use of land. Landowners are able to charge non-landowners for the use of their property because land is in fixed supply and it can be used in the production of goods. The form of the rental payment, whether it be money, labour or surplus product, depended on the society. This type of rent is the oldest and it used to be the only kind. Rent has historically been associated with land and the story of how this association was broken, at least in the mainstream, is important for the development of modern rent theory.

There are at least three distinct approaches to land rent in the history of economic thought: these can be identified as the Ricardian approach, the marginalist/neoclassical approach and the Sraffian approach.[15] Each approach is informed by the prevailing views on value at the time. Ricardian rent is a form of surplus paid to the owner of land that derives from the differing fertility or natural properties of land. Marginalist rent is considered the difference between marginal product and opportunity cost of any factor of production – i.e., the marginal product of labour is the change in output occasioned by the application of one extra unit of labour to the production process. The opportunity cost of adding that labour is deducted from the output and the result is rent. A farmer, for example, might put on another labourer for the day whose wages cost $100 in order to help pick more avocados which increase profits by $150. The economic rent here would be $50. The marginalist view describes rent through the sphere of exchange, using the movements of price in markets for factors of production to explain how rents arise. This is contrary to the Ricardian view which saw rent as a surplus to be explained in the sphere of production. The rationale for this change was that Ricardian rents and the productivist explanation failed to account for scarcity, which is best explained in markets where supply and demand can be held in relation to one another. Finally, Sraffian rent theory shows that Ricardian rent and its productivist approach can indeed explain scarcity, not as a natural attribute of land but rather as a function of the competition for land between produced goods, like machinery.

The idea that rent is the reward for the ownership of land and for permitting its use in production is built on a foundation of a particular view of how society functions. There are three factors of production – land, labour and capital – and three groups or classes of people correspond to these factors – landowners, wage labourers and capitalists. Landowners receive rent for permitting the use of their land, labourers receive wages for contributing their labour and capitalists receive profit or interest for investing their capital. This stylized view of how society functions is the foundation for a theory of rent that is usually associated with a 'classical' approach, owing to its association with David Ricardo and others in the so-called classical school of political economy. The who and the what questions about land rent have been answered in brief, but how exactly do we determine how much rent is paid?

The first thing to consider with land rent is what possible uses are there for land? Some obvious uses are for extractive industry, like mining, for agriculture, or for construction of buildings, like houses or factories. These uses are in competition with one another. That is to say that the choice to do one necessarily precludes the option to do the others. The competing uses for land means that for some, rent serves a positive social function because its level signals what uses for land are most desired. This approach corresponds broadly to the neoclassical or marginalist view because it operates on assumptions about the allocation of scarce resources among competing ends.

A different view to the social function of rents is expressed by the so-called 'classical' approach. In this view, landowners receive rents not for any productive activity but rather as a passive form of income purely on the basis of ownership of the scarce resource land. This view was expressed by some during the Corn Laws debates in the United Kingdom in the nineteenth century where landowners were considered social parasites, receiving unearned wealth solely on the basis of inherited titles to land bestowed from the feudal system. The implication of this argument is that landowners as a social class were no longer necessary in a system of competitive capitalism, where productive contributions to society were rewarded based on merit. This is certainly what some of the most trenchant critics of landowners, like David Ricardo, claimed during the Corn Laws debates. Others, like Thomas Robert Malthus, famously opposed Ricardo's view, supporting landlords while raising some of the thornier issues around what the relationship between population growth and food supply means for policy.

The mechanism by which rent is seen to be a brake on social progress is instructive for demonstrating the details of how land rent is determined. If we accept that land is a finite resource and that its use requires choices to be made about which alternative is most required in society, then the issue of population growth presents a particular problem. Population growth increases the demand for food. The need for more food places pressure on land that is already being used to produce food, as well as increasing the incentives to take more land under cultivation. Land already under culti-vation requires more *intensive* use while land not yet under cultivation is said to be at the *extensive* margin.

Population growth might indicate social progress as increased production allows more people to consume goods and services. If the demand for land increases, under normal conditions, then so too could the charge for access to land, or land rent, go up. This means that as more and more land is taken into cultivation, the power of landowners to increase rents grows also. So, too, would the price of food rise as less desirable land is used for food production, meaning that wages would also need to increase to cover the rising cost of food. If both rents and wages increase, profits must decline in proportion, unless productivity increases. Wages can only ever be as low as it costs workers to ensure they can, well, go to work. This means that the level of subsistence sets the wage level. If rents increase as the population grows, requiring more food production, and wages must remain at subsistence levels, there comes a point when capitalists can no longer realize a profit. At this point, there would be no incentive for capitalists to invest in agriculture, and population growth, and hence social progress, would stop. According to this view, landowners are a brake on social progress because although they do not contribute to production, they reap an income from ownership that takes away from the incomes of the productive classes, labourers and capitalists.

Resource curse, Dutch disease and rent policy

Resource rents refer to payments for the use of natural resources but the issue is complicated by the intersection of the two meanings of rent that prompted the *Economist* to label rent 'confusing'. There are two important considerations for mineral rent: the payment for access to minerals, and the ways in which the level of rent is determined. In other words, how much and for what reason is a rent being paid? The usual framing of mineral rents is in something called a bid rent, where a firm is pitted against a government in a bidding-type situation. It is generally assumed that minerals are owned by the government on behalf of citizens. Whatever the case may be, the owner of the minerals permits access to their resources for a rental payment. The determination of how much rent is paid depends on several factors. The quality of the minerals is important, along with how much it would cost to 'produce', or extract, the mineral deposits. Any costs associated with bringing the product to market for sale are also taken into consideration. As a general rule, the amount of rent can be identified by the sale price for the commodity minus cost of production plus the average rate of profit in that industry. So, for example, if 1 tonne of iron ore sold for $100 and it cost $50 to extract, transport and sell the ore in an industry where profits average $20 per tonne, the rent would be $30 per tonne.

Much of the discussion on mineral rents is dominated by the issue of exhaustibility. The classic study that opened this field of inquiry in mainstream economics was Harold Hotelling's 1931 article on the 'economics of exhaustible resources'. In it, Hotelling sought to integrate variables of time, depletion of finite supply and the level of information available to market actors to derive basic principles for understanding the 'peculiar problems of mineral wealth'.[16] The basic problem is intuitive. If there is a finite supply of minerals, how do we know how much they are worth now relative to some unknowable future? For example, is it worth digging up more coal today to burn for electricity generation or should we leave it buried because of the expected future costs of emitting greenhouse gases? The problem of exhaustibility cascaded into the discourse of 'peak oil' in the 1970s where publications like *The Limits to Growth*, commissioned by the Club of Rome, set the tone for a new generation of people concerned with the consequences of depleting stocks of finite resources. The links between the study of rents in extractive industry and issues of ecological degradation and sustainability are apparent. Less clear are the ways in which the methodological underpinnings of arguments like Hotelling's constrain the latitude for thinking through these complex problems. The issue of mineral rent read through the lens of exhaustibility is one prime example of how framing the problem of rent in terms of scarce resources allocated between competing ends boils the problem down to whether the resource should be used. Whether this framing is sufficient for grappling with the nuances of problems of sustainability is up for debate. It could be argued, for example, that it is precisely because fossil fuels cannot be exhausted without setting off ecological calamity that Hotelling's framework is incompatible with sustainability.

Another area in which mineral rent features prominently is in the distribution of gains from extractive industry in the global economy. The organization of global extractive industry is an important topic of study for various reasons. Land-based commodity production is vitally important for satisfying basic subsistence needs like food and shelter. Furthermore, the spillover effects of reliance upon industries engaged in primary extractivism have been shown to have mixed results for national economies. There is a long-standing debate in economics about the relationship between economic development and the types of industry prevailing in a country. Those who subscribe to liberal trade theory advocate free trade among countries where each country specializes in the types of production in which they have a comparative advantage. Countries that have an abundance of mineral wealth, for example, would be better off, according to liberal trade theory, specializing in extractive industry and exporting their minerals in exchange for processed goods produced elsewhere. Governments in countries that have abundant mineral reserves should, in theory, be able to charge high rents for access to their minerals and therefore distribute the gains from this 'gift of nature' to their citizens. The logic of this argument is compelling, but the empirical data seem to indicate a perverse reality. Some studies claim that countries that have land in abundance, relative to capital and labour, tend to be less developed according to several measures. Much of the poverty that exists in the world currently, for example, is concentrated in regions where countries rely primarily on the production of land-based commodities. This apparent contradiction has been referred to as the paradox of plenty or the resource curse.

Defining rent?

Heterodox rent theory draws on interdisciplinary insights and methods to substantiate its general criticism of the mainstream approach to rent. A notion of rent derived from the interaction of supply and demand in markets for factors of production is limited in its capacity to explain the social significance of the rental payment beyond the allocative investment function that neoclassical theory claims rent serves. Heterodox approaches emphasize the material characteristics of rent-generating assets, the property rights that give assets meaning in markets and the social consequences of rent extraction and appropriation. Rent according to mainstream economics is a question of efficient resource allocation and the degree of competition in markets for factors of production. The political economy critique of mainstream rent theory shows that there is more to rent, particularly issues of social power as a function of property rights in capitalism. Just as in the previous chapter on the mainstream approach to rent theory, heterodox approaches are compiled in Figure 4.1 below to provide a point of reference for the discussion above.

While heterodox rent theory articulates clear lines of critique of the mainstream approach, there are also points of agreement that are important to note. Namely, the notion that rent can apply to more than just land is key to understanding the various differences between the heterodox and the mainstream, as well as disagreements within heterodox approaches.

The question of neat definitions of rent according to the different approaches could be refined to account for the variegation and shared intellectual heritages of the approaches surveyed in this chapter. Rather than distinct conceptions of rent, there are contending points of emphasis for the most part which line up alongside one end of a deep divide which considers rent to be a question of land, or not. How we got to this point was the subject of discussion in chapter 2. Why these contending views matter will be the main questions informing the discussion in chapter 5.

Before moving onto those questions, it is necessary, from a purely practical perspective, to arrive at a provisional understanding of rent. The next chapter seeks to elaborate the reasons why the study of rent today is important, so there needs to be a shorthand for what rent means that does not require the detailed examination of the contending approaches surveyed above. Various approaches to understanding rent have been listed already so there is no need for repetition, but there are some common themes which could be used as categories of rent going forward. One question

Figure 4.1 Heterodox (non-neoclassical) rent theory

Type of rent	Brief definition	Source of rent	Examples
World mining rent	Rent that should be paid to owners of minerals but rather is appropriated by multinational mining companies that own and control access to technology, finance, machinery and skilled labour	Social power of multinational mining companies	Relative poverty of Nigeria compared to Norway despite both owning and selling the same commodity, oil
SoP (systems of provision) rent	Payment for the use of land to those who own and control access to vertically integrated systems required for the production and consumption of commodity groups	Landed property and the upstream and downstream activities where the effects of capitalist landed property can reverberate	The value of cobalt that should be paid to citizens of the Democratic Republic of Congo where it is mined but is instead paid to Apple and Samsung who use it in their batteries
Technoscience rent	Forms of economic rent that are paid for the use of outputs of technological and scientific innovations	The structures and processes of technoscientific capitalism mediated by scarcity and property rights	Uber fares, digital media subscriptions, time spent ignoring advertisements on internet pages
Differential ground rent	Surplus payments owing to differing fertility of land or from the differing applications of capital	Differing fertility of land or differing investments of capital on land of equal fertility	The price of red wine from Bordeaux relative to the cost of red wine from Moldova
Absolute ground rent	Payment for the extension of production onto new lands of better or worse quality than existing productive land	Class monopoly control of landed property	The cost of access to the moon paid by Tesla for setting up mining operations
Patriarchal rent seeking	Men exploiting the relative efficiency of women specializing in reproductive labour beyond the realm of birth to create hierarchies in society that obstruct the reorganization of the household division of labour	The emergence of hierarchy on the basis of short-lived efficiencies in the specialization of women in reproductive labour	Gender wage gaps
Ecological rent	The amount of natural resources used in production that exceeds what is necessary to maintain output using optimal allocation of all resources – i.e., the carbon footprint above net zero emissions	Absolute scarcity of some natural resources leading to binding resource constraints such as the capacity for ecosystems to absorb carbon emissions	Carbon emissions beyond net zero after 2050 in China and the USA

that could be asked of all the heterodox approaches to rent, so called because of their explicit opposition to neoclassical rent theory, is whether there is an alternative conception of rent put forward or if the scope of analysis of extant rent theory is instead expanded to include novel contexts.

The examples of rent considered from both the mainstream and heterodox approaches suggest that there are a couple of main ideas to consider when looking at types of rent and the ways in which they are conceived. One way to distinguish these themes is along the lines of how they explain or understand rent. One approach focuses mainly on the thing that rent is paid for. That is, this approach emphasizes the 'thing-ness' of rent by tethering the explanation of rent to a specific type of property bound up in a historically specific system of property rights, a commodity. The rent paid for the use of land is a land rent, for labour, a labour rent and so on. *Commodity-based rent theory* might well be an appropriate way to characterize this line of reasoning.

The other approach, while also acknowledging that rent is paid for commodities, sets about explaining the existence of rent based on how that commodity comes to be exchanged. In this view, rent arises during the process of exchange and can be identified through the formation of prices. Indeed, according to this approach, rent itself is determined by price. The context within which price formation and exchange occurs is, at least in this framework of knowledge, the market. More importantly, though, for the concept of economic rent is the fact that the degree of competition in the market not only determines the level of rent but is the very basis for it. A perfectly competitive market eliminates economic rent according to neoclassical rent theory because there would be no reason to purchase factors of production above their equilibrium price. For this reason, this approach might well be characterized as *competition-based rent theory*.

Both approaches attempt to understand the same thing but through different avenues of inquiry. It makes sense then that there would be overlaps and points of intersection. It would be difficult, for example, to conceive of a rent being paid for the use of some type of commodity, like land, in the twenty-first century removed entirely from the influence of land markets. Discussions of rental prices for housing are almost always carried on in the context of what is happening in the real-estate market. Likewise with technology-based industry and the rents generated by virtue of holding patents on intellectual property. It is hard to think about Samsung battling Apple over battery technology if it were not regarding attempts to increase market share for their smartphones. The key point of distinction remains, however, that one view sees competition in markets as the source of rents while the other contends that it is the commodity itself, and the property rights ascribed to it, that generates the rents.

Does this make much of a difference when twenty-first-century capitalist societies are in question? After all, any capitalist society today is dominated by markets when it comes to the ways in which commodities are produced, exchanged, distributed and even consumed. Take food, for example. The production of food staples, like corn, wheat and rice, takes place in a truly world-scale industrial context. Firms ranging from boutique small-scale operators making artisanal cheeses in the rolling hills of Andalucía right through to broadacre corn farms stretching west from Iowa are connected through global markets where the prices for their products and the things they need to produce them are determined.

Does it really matter if rents arise from the character of the commodity and the property rights within which it is embedded for which rents are paid or if they emerge due to the degree of competition in the market within which they are exchanged? Particularly when it seems that today one cannot be taken without the other. A corn fritter topped with queso payoyo, bought and savoured in a London gastropub, will contain elements of rent in its price that derive from its commodity form but also, inescapably, from the degree of competition in the markets where the things needed to make it were bought. Even if the corn was grown in the organic vegetable patch on the roof of the Soho townhouse-turned-pub while the goats milked for the cheese have grazed on clover in St Anne's Churchyard down the road, the relative price of artisan goods is still affected by what the Round-up-resistant GMO corn from Nebraska fetches when sold to goat-feed lots in Granada.

The source of rent does matter, though. Rentiers are the benefactors of unearned gains. Even those who dispute that this is the key problem of rent admit that it is the dearth of competition that generates rents which make it a problematic, or indeed undesirable, element of modern political economies.[17] Whichever way the problem of rent is considered, there appears to be a broad consensus, with a few important exceptions, that it is an unwanted problem. To make it go away requires a very precise understanding of where it comes from.

Two categories capable of grouping together contending approaches to rent are commodity-based and competition-based rents. These categories refer to the fact that some approaches to rent claim they derive from, and are mediated by, the characteristics of specific types of asset or property. It appears, for example, that economic rent differs from the more general type of rent surveyed above in chapter 1 in relation to housing in a couple of important ways. Whereas rent in the former sense hinges upon the commodity as its basis, the latter concept of economic rent, coming out of neoclassical theory but also deployed in heterodox approaches such as with technoscience rent, is agnostic about its material tether and more dependent on the degree of competition in the market in which it is exchanged. Economic rent is therefore a function of competition while rent is considered a function of commodities. The various forms of rent discussed thus far might be considered as nodes along the arc of a pendulum with its points of reflux at commodity and competition. Figure 4.2 below visualizes what this arc might look like.

Commodity-based rent refers to the fact that the rental payment for the use of a resource is a function of the commodity. The commodity in this context refers to property, a thing, tangible or not, that is produced and that someone possesses, within the context of a system of property rights. The basis of rent for this commodity is its material character but the reason that it produces rent for its owner at all is due to the system of property rights within which its ownership, control, exchange and consumption is determined. This is why 'commodity' is the most appropriate descriptor for this category of rent, rather than say 'property' or 'asset',[18] because the commodity encompasses both the materiality of

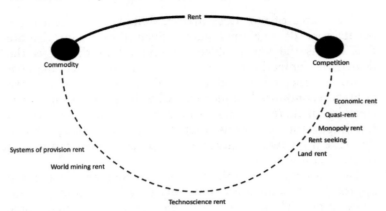

Figure 4.2

the thing and its cocoon of property rights which are histori-cally specific.

Competition-based rent refers to what is known in the mainstream as economic rent. It is tethered to competition because the rental payment in this case derives from the degree of competition in the market where the factor of production in question is purchased. Competition is preferred to market as a descriptor for this type of rent because the rent arises within a market but only insofar as it is a function of the degree of competition present. The rationale is not merely to put new labels on the same concepts but rather to illuminate the limits of the orthodoxy where the space for alternatives that reveal the social character of rent beyond its capacity for allocating scarce resources between competing ends begins. An iceberg analogy could be useful, wherein rent is the totality of the iceberg and mainstream rent theory illuminates what is above the surface, whereas political economy approaches to rent throw a spotlight on what keeps the edifice of the rental payment afloat. Figure 4.3 sketches what this iceberg might look like, showing that even when using the neoclassical concept of rent, which cannot offer a notion of rent distinct from other factor incomes, as a point of departure, the political economy critique can open new avenues of inquiry to reveal what socio-economic factors undergird the rental payment.

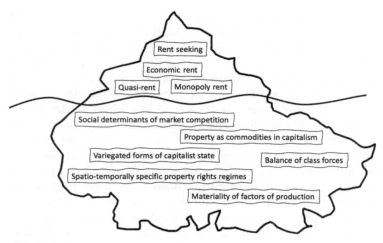

Rent seeking

Economic rent

Quasi-rent   Monopoly rent

Social determinants of market competition

Property as commodities in capitalism

Variegated forms of capitalist state

Balance of class forces

Spatio-temporally specific property rights regimes

Materiality of factors of production

Figure 4.3

The crux of this debate rests on the claim that economic theory is capable of constructing a notion of rent that distinguishes it from other factor incomes, like wages and profit, only if it recognizes a distinct role for landed property.[19] Or, to put this another way, how can a theory of rent be distinguished from a theory of wages or a theory of profit and interest – the forms of revenues that factors of production receive as incomes – if the concept of economic rent can arise with all factors, not just land? If wages are the factor income to owners of labour, how can they also receive rents as a revenue for selling their labour? Why is there a need for a theory of wages if the theory of economic rent can account for the income derived from the sale of labour?

This view proposes that there are specific effects of landed property that intervene in the operation of an economy that are not generalizable to the theories of capital and labour as they relate to the operation of the economy. The emphasis here is on the fact that land is subsumed into a system of property rights, rather than the material elements of the land itself. It is the property rights that act as the proxy for the interaction of land in the economy. While the material elements of land are obviously important, it is the quality of being property, which takes the form of a commodity in capitalism, that makes landed property distinctive compared to capital and labour. The key question here, which is yet to be satisfactorily resolved in the big debates on rent theory, is whether rent theory should be specific to land or if it can be generalized across the other factors of production.

There is no one-liner to explain the complexity of rent. The essential dilemma is that rent is a concept developed by people to help understand how their societies function in relation to their surroundings. Given that these societies are characterized by complex divisions of labour, constituted by autonomous beings enmeshed in webs of relationships they themselves cannot fully control, forming part of an ecology they do not fully understand, it is no wonder there is contention, controversy and confusion about rent. The next chapter discusses three important reasons to study rent today.

5
Why is Rent Important Today?

We have so far reflected on two questions about rent. Chapters 1–4 surveyed key approaches to understanding rent from the mainstream and heterodox perspectives, both historical and current – i.e., what is rent and how did we get to this point in rent theory? The short answer is that the meaning of rent is disputed and cannot be boiled down to one generally accepted view. Whether rent is a revenue unique to owners of landed property or is an income generated by scarcity, real or contrived, that accrues to owners of any productive property in the absence of competition is one way to distinguish the broad orientations in rent theory. The former tends to be associated with more obscure traditions in heterodox economic thought while the latter enjoys wide acceptance across both mainstream rent theory and its critics. At stake in these debates on rent are how and why rent is a problem in twenty-first-century societies and what, if anything, should be done about it. This final chapter asks why rent is important today. The first section looks at the way rent has featured in the big social processes that have created the present state of things in global political economy: globalization, neo-liberalism and financialization. The creation and capture of rent has been an important driver of recent historical developments and is important for understanding meta-narratives shaping the present. Does it continue to be so and for what reasons? The last section offers some thoughts on this question, identifying current hot topics in rent theory and speculating about how these debates might bear on understanding the social forces driving global capitalism into the future.

There are at least three good reasons for sharpening our conception of rent today. Creating and capturing rents is essential to concerns about economic inequality, ecology and economic dynamism. Levels of economic inequality are driven by how the value of the products created by the activity of most people is siphoned off in various ways by the relatively few people who control access to them. The capacity for communities around the world to develop in ways that satisfy not just basic needs but also aspirational wants likewise depends in large part on the ability to access resources which can in turn be used to produce goods and services. Underlying all of this is the challenge, in which the entire world is involved, to avert a climate crisis by reimagining and reorganizing the way we interact with each other in relation to our surroundings. The issues of economic dynamism, economic inequality and the threat posed by anthropocentric climate change are suffused by rent. Big global problems affecting all of us are in some way caused by, or are consequences of, the creation and capture of rental revenues. But are rents inherently problematic? Or are rents to be tolerated, managed or perhaps even encouraged?

Rent has long been considered an unearned gain received by those who have done little to deserve the wealth and privilege usually associated with rentier incomes. Landlords have been the subject of contempt in various societies historically and more recently. This is especially the case in places like the United Kingdom, with a long history of land ownership being concentrated in the hands of a relatively small proportion of the population whose wealth is at least perceived to derive primarily from being born into the right family rather than as a reward for hard graft. This aspect of the rent question, of fairness and of just deserts, is one obvious consideration for judging the significance of rent studies in twenty-first-century political economy. There is no shortage of analyses that set out to put the boot into the privileged rentiers of the world. The prospect of being able to reap rewards without any productive contribution to society might well be considered undesirable because if enough people can do so, economic dynamism – i.e., the potential for economic growth – might stall. On the other hand, many would relish the prospect of receiving income simply by virtue of owning things, rather than having to work. Why else would the lottery exist? Aside from rentiers defying the deeply ingrained ethos of getting out what you put in under capitalism, what else is important or problematic about rent today?

There is growing disquiet that more than the aspirations of workers to be freed from the yoke of waged labour, there is a major restructuring of global capitalism underway that poses serious problems for most people. A report published by UNCTAD in 2017 spells out this concern, claiming that 'what is new in this debate is not so much a preoccupation with "bad apples" or the use of potentially abusive practices by individual firms in isolation.' Rather, the report goes on to say, 'it is the concern that increasing market concentration in leading sectors of the global economy and the growing market and lobbying powers of dominant corporations are creating a new form of global rentier capitalism to the detriment of balanced and inclusive growth for the many.'[1]

The debate mentioned here is an old one. Is bigger necessarily better when it comes to producers, and what are the consequences for competition in markets? These questions have preoccupied those interested in political economy since the beginning of capitalism. The shift in thinking from these problems being isolated instances of firm behaviour to now considering if this is a systemic feature of the global economy, however, are not as new as this excerpt might suggest. As this report itself makes clear, concerns about the lack of attention paid to power relations and the structural effects of the growing market domination and lobbying powers of large corporations were raised several decades ago by people like Raul Prebisch, the first secretary of UNCTAD. Prebisch is famous for writing the *Principal Problems of Development in Latin America* report published in 1950 which became the road map for three decades of import-substitution-industrialization, often referred to as protectionism, on that continent, although the extent of concentration of ownership and control in the vertically and horizontally integrated systems that provide food, medicines and clothing today might have made even Raul Prebisch blush.

There are clear moral grounds for being critical of rentiers alongside less apparent and more objective reasons – i.e., rentier capitalism might be bad for society, irrespective of how we feel about it. Or, to put it another way, the core problem of rent might not be about fairness but rather it could be that a society organized around the imperative of capturing rent is unsustainable. Capitalism, with its rentier inflection, could pose a danger to itself because the compulsion to engage in activities that produce surplus, the vital driver of capitalism, is precisely the tendency that capturing and creating rents retards. The study of rent today is therefore important because at least three major social problems of the twenty-first century are either caused by, or are consequences of, creating and capturing rental revenue.

A growing chorus of scholars is drawing attention to the emergence of a new and problematic form of rentier capitalism, defined in opposition to egalitarian notions of balanced and inclusive growth for the many. This suggests that the problem of rent may not be confined to, or be explained sufficiently by, its conception as an allocative mechanism for investment or as an index of market power in markets for factors of production, as mainstream rent theory claims. The issue is not so much that mainstream rent theory does not allow for constructing the problem of rentier capitalism, as the UNCTAD report frames it – i.e., a problem of monopoly and competition in leading sectors of the global economy driving up inequality. The mainstream notion of rent seeking, for example, is precisely about the capacity for powerful firms to lobby governments to manipulate competition in markets they operate in. The conclusion, however, of an examination of rent seeking using neoclassical economics is that governments are not able to anticipate market mechanisms and should therefore minimize their distorting interference in markets that operate best when firms and people are free to choose. A free and perfectly competitive market, according to neoclassical economics, does not generate rents. What the UNCTAD report suggests is that we are perhaps entering new terrain where stylized notions of competition might have been superseded, requiring the formulation of new ways to comprehend how rents are created and captured.

The rationale for a more critical and comprehensive study of rent is made up of two elements: motivation and focus. The motivations are moral and objective. Questions of justice, fairness and ethics are clearly relevant to the study of rent but so too are avenues of inquiry that emphasize the logical consequences of particular social arrangements in objective and dispassionate terms, to the extent that such analyses of social phenomena are possible. The focus of rent is potentially extensive, given what we know about the contending approaches to rent theory, but it could usefully be confined to three major problems confronting social scientists today: economic inequality, anthropocentric climate crisis and stalling economic dynamism. Figure 5.1 below depicts how these three areas of focus constitute what some consider to be a new and emerging mode of social organization called rentier capitalism. Potential themes and motivations related to these derivative problems of rent are contained within the locus of inquiry possible within a political economy approach to rent, represented in this diagram by the broken line.

Rent and economic inequality

Economic inequality is comprised of two measures: wealth and income. Wealth is a stock of assets whereas income designates a flow of revenue. Assets are property which

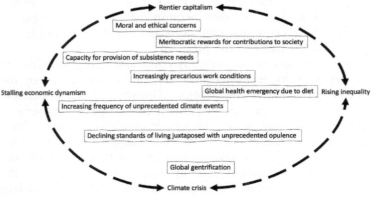

Figure 5.1

are valuable, or worth money, and revenues are income streams. Amazon CEO Jeff Bezos is estimated to have a net worth – i.e., the total market value of all financial and non-financial assets minus outstanding liabilities – of US$187.5 billion,[2] while making about US$13.4 million an hour.[3] The former is wealth, the latter is income. Wealth is made up of assets, or property, typically distinguished between physical (machinery, factories, houses, tractors) and financial (government bonds, cash, crypto currency) assets. Income is the revenue received for permitting the use of assets owned. This use of assets can be productive or not. Bezos earning a salary paid by Amazon for services rendered as its CEO is an income received in return for expending labour. This is considered a productive contribution insofar as the output of that labour is measurable in the system of national accounts in the United States where Amazon is listed on the American Stock Exchange, or NYSE American as it is known today. That income would therefore be called a wage. The income Bezos receives from the share portfolio he owns would be considered rent because its source was ownership of a financial asset. Had Bezos sold some of these shares and then invested the money from the sale into the purchase of land in China to build a new Amazon warehouse, the income received from this investment would be considered interest and profit. Debate continues about whether income or wealth inequality is the more problematic, but there is general agreement that levels of economic inequality at present in most countries is not sustainable. Rent features prominently in the attempts to explain how economic inequality has got so bad and in the potential solutions to the problem.

Rent seeking is, as previously discussed, the lobbying of government by firms to intervene in the operation of the market to minimize competition. The absence of competition concentrates market power and therefore generates returns above what they would be under conditions approaching perfect competition. These above-average returns are called rents and the firm behaviour that creates them is called rent seeking. In the mainstream approach to rent theory, the source of the problem is that government actors themselves are distorting the operations of markets at the behest of firms and for their personal gain. This is why rent seeking is typically associated with government corruption and the inefficiency of bureaucracy. In the heterodox approach to rent, the mechanism by which rent seeking occurs is the same but the problem is seen to lie not in the notion that governments distort the operation of markets, but rather that markets themselves are imperfect and that the government has a role to play in eradicating the rent-seeking opportunities. While the mainstream and its critics agree that rent seeking is undesirable, the means to solve the problem lie in opposing solutions that reflect the normative foundations of their approaches, or how they imagine the world should operate.

The examination of rising levels of economic inequality in the twenty-first century has identified rent seeking as one of its main drivers. The UNCTAD report above notes increasing market concentration in leading sectors of the global economy, alongside growing lobbying and market powers of corporations, as ushering in a new form of rentier capitalism. This new society is one where rent seeking becomes the norm rather than the exception and those who pursue such behaviour, rentiers, have become so powerful that even governments that are not corrupt face difficulties in challenging their actions. The issue depicted here is basically a battle between powerful multinational corporations and sovereign national governments. The campaign for a global digital services tax is one example that bears out how this conflict occurs. Britain, alongside other countries in Europe, renewed efforts to design and implement a global digital services tax in 2020 that would charge companies like Google, Facebook and Amazon a levy for revenues earned in their countries. Talks on the issue organized by the OECD stalled when US Treasury Secretary, Steven Mnuchin, withdrew from discussions, citing the lack of progress on the policy design as the reason.[4] The move angered those involved in the process who had been working towards finalizing negotiations by the end of 2020. The underlying reasons for Mnuchin's actions have not been disclosed but it is easy to see how the global digital tax might not be seen as aligning with the interests of the US Treasury. Amazon, Google and Facebook are all US-based firms. Mnuchin might have thought that they may get even less tax in the United States if the firms were required to pay more taxes overseas.

Another way that rent seeking is seen to drive economic inequality is through the lobbying of government by the wealthiest citizens, as opposed to corporations, to legislate in favour of their interests. The lobbying of government, for example, to preference tax cuts to the wealthy to promote investment as the driver of economic growth is one example. Much of the push for austerity regimes in several countries in the wake of the global financial crisis (GFC) and leading up to the current Covid-19-induced crisis can be seen in the context of rent-seeking behaviour by wealthy citizens. Laws that enable the wealthy to hold onto their wealth and to increase their stock of income-generating assets are also seen to be potentially linked to rent seeking. This account goes some way to explaining the emergence of a housing crisis in some countries where homeownership is becoming less affordable for more people because those who own houses can use the income generated from these assets to purchase more housing stock, pushing up demand for housing and therefore bidding up prices. Laws that allow investors to make tax deductions on their investment losses, like 'negative gearing' laws, are one example of where successful lobbying by the wealthiest in society have kept legislation in place that most people might consider to be undesirable or unfair.

Ecology, rent and the climate crisis

Launching their *Making Peace with Nature* report in April 2021, United Nations Environmental Programme (UNEP) executive director Ingrid Andersen said the 'three planetary crises' of climate change, biodiversity loss and pollution are reinforcing one another and driving further damage to the environment and our health.[5] The report states that the 'exploitation of nature has reached unsustainable levels and is undermining the Earth's capacity to sustain human well-being' while 'human prosperity is strained by widening inequalities, whereby the burden of environmental decline weighs heaviest on the poor and vulnerable.'[6] The Sustainable Development Goals (SDGs) are the policy-oriented infrastructure through

which the United Nations (UN) aims to facilitate international cooperation to ameliorate these crises. Attempts to
make sense of these connected and mutually reinforcing
processes have proliferated in the social sciences since at
least 1972, when the UN hosted its first conference on
sustainable development in Stockholm, in which the UNEP
was created. Radical green movements during that decade
spawned, or at least motivated, studies of the limitations of
capitalist production on earth, such as the famous *Limits
to Growth*. Since that time, environmentally oriented social
movements and scholarship have developed sophisticated
modes of inquiry to investigate the causes and consequences
of ecological degradation. Rent features prominently in this
discourse.

Two of the planetary crises cited by Andersen are inextricably linked. The pace at which climate change proceeds and
its level are determined in great measure by the amount of
pollution that can occur. The key driver is the emission of greenhouse gases, namely carbon dioxide. One avenue of scholarly
inquiry that has attempted to address this problem deploys the
notion of a Ricardian rent to capture an 'ecological rent' by
making carbon emissions a resource. If carbon emissions are
considered a resource within the framework of neoclassical
production theory, it too must be allocated efficiently through
markets. As the optimum allocation of carbon emissions is
net zero – i.e., the amount of carbon dioxide emitted is equal
to the amount of carbon dioxide captured and taken out of
the atmosphere – any level of emissions above this is rent –
i.e., a surplus above what is necessary to deploy and use a
resource. The point of this framing is to show that economic
production or demand that overshoots 'biocapacity'[7]– i.e.,
the productivity of ecological assets, especially the capacity
to absorb carbon emissions – can be conceived and measured
as an economic cost.[8] Using this approach, any proposed
infrastructure developments in a metropolis like London, for
example, could be subject to an ecological rent test, whereby
approvals could depend on showing that the carbon emissions
created during construction and operation of the infrastructure could be offset by technologies built into the project.
Transport is the largest source of carbon emissions in the
United Kingdom, accounting for 34% of the total, primarily

generated by petrol and diesel use in road transport.[9] The UK Committee on Climate Change forecasts that to achieve net zero, there need to be 46 million electric vehicles on UK roads by 2050.[10] If the total amount of emissions generated in the making and maintenance of the 46 million electric cars and their associated infrastructure equalled the emissions that currently account for 34% of the UK total, there would be no ecological rent. This approach to rent is firmly within the mainstream in that its innovation is to bring carbon emissions into markets through imputing an economic cost. Once there, the market mechanisms that determine rents – i.e., competition, scarcity relative to demand and distortion through external intervention – work themselves out but for the optimum allocation of emissions, net zero. It is an elegant proposal for an important social problem that demonstrates the analytical power of the mainstream approach to rent theory.

Another perspective on rent that engages with planetary ecological crises is the value-grabbing notion of rent that comes out of political ecology. Value grabbing designates the struggle over the capture of rents as a form of surplus value. This concept is an attempt to distinguish between the process of capital accumulation, wherein surplus value is produced, and that of value grabbing, where the surplus value produced in the accumulation process is captured in the context of a distributional struggle.[11] This perspective draws on the historical materialist tradition where the contestation over rent is carried out by distinct classes, or fractions of classes, in society. Two distinct historical moments are empha-sized in this approach: the moment that property rights are created, and the moment in which the struggle to appropriate the rents derived from those property rights plays out. In countries where a process of colonization and decolonization has occurred, for example, the changing character of the governance institutions can create or destroy property rights to land and therefore directly affect who owns, and therefore receives benefits from, the land. Radical land reforms in 1974 during the Ethiopian civil war, for example, enshrined land in its constitution as the 'common property of the people' and 'owned by the state'. The legacy of this ambiguity is that the state in Ethiopia today grants 49-year leases to foreign and domestic investors who displace residents to reap the benefits of their income-generating assets.[12] This approach is an example of historical materialist rent theory that emphasizes monopoly rather than landed property and insists that rent is a purely distributional concern rather than something capable of affecting the patterns of capital accumulation. The benefit of this approach is that it spotlights the complicated dimensions of class power refracted through the state apparatus and class fractions. This is especially the case when considering decolonial contexts where there are several groups vying for the capture of rent and jockeying for control of the state. This applicability to the poorest and most populace places in the world makes this emphasis on the class struggles over rent particularly useful for understanding what the UNEP characterizes as the disproportionate burden on low-income countries when it comes to dealing with the planetary ecological crisis.

Global rentier capitalism and economic dynamism

In their famous 1848 *Manifesto of the Communist Party*, Karl Marx and Frederick Engels praise the bourgeoisie as having 'accomplished wonders far surpassing Egyptian pyramids, Roman aqueducts, and Gothic Cathedrals; it has conducted expeditions that put in the shade all former Exoduses of nations and crusades'. It is, according to Marx and Engels, the 'constant revolutionising of production, uninterrupted disturbance of all social conditions, everlasting uncertainty and agitation [that] distinguish the bourgeois epoch from all earlier ones.'[13] This is a far cry from the rentier capitalism that some argue prevails today where the rentier opts for a 'quiet life', focused on 'sweating existing income-generating assets – shoring up defences arrayed around them, fighting any attempts to stem the flows of money they elicit – rather than, for example, innovating in the interests of developing new products or services'.[14] The dynamism of capitalism that even its fiercest critics lauded is now under threat, according to recent scholarship that has sought to understand twenty-first-century society through the lens of rent theory.

The UNCTAD report cited above emphasized the concentration of market power in leading sectors of the global economy as well as the growing lobbying power of major corporations as detrimental to the goal of balanced and inclusive growth for the many. Two dimensions of the critique of rentierism are evident in this appraisal: the moral and the objective. The moral critique is evident in the fact that balance and inclusivity are emphasized in relation to growth. The character of economic growth is therefore imbued with a moral character. But economic growth in and of itself does not necessarily need to be guided by ethical or moral concerns. Indeed, the history of capitalism provides ample evidence to the contrary. The second, and perhaps more important dimension, for the purposes of this section at least, is that rentier capitalism impedes economic growth. When firms derive income primarily from the benefits that ownership of assets confers and less so from the productive contribution of labour, the effect of this approach becoming generalized across the economy would be to stifle productivity. Rather than firms producing more to promote economic growth, they would merely be drawing incomes away from other firms through payments for access to capital – i.e., goods or services used to produce other goods or services. The overall effect of capitalism in which the largest and most powerful firms prioritized income streams that captured rents rather than production for profits would be economic stagnation, rather than economic dynamism. Several studies have sought to refine and expand this general rentier capitalism thesis.

One element of the rentier capitalism thesis emphasizes inequitable distribution of income because of the formation of a global rentier elite which is aided significantly by institutions of government that are supposed to be guarding against such self-serving behaviour. A rentier economy, in this view, is one where more than 40% of income is derived from economic rents.[15] The United States has reached this point and is seen as one example where industries like finance have come to rely on a business model which seeks to generate rents through the purchase of income-generating assets, rather than through productive investment. Banks and financial firms led this charge historically but were joined by non-financial firms like General Electric in the lead up to 2008. Corporate lobbying of successive governments in the United States since at least the 1980s has led to interest-rate liberalization, reduced costs of capital mobility, increased returns to foreign financial investment and decreasing real wages. Low wage growth coupled with asset price inflation has meant that more people rely on debt-fuelled consumption to subsist. Financiers sought to increase their rental incomes by lending recklessly to as many people as possible and then bundling up these loans into investment products which are assets sold to other financial firms where debt repayments become rental incomes.[16] The GFC is cited as an example of what happens when such behaviour becomes endemic. Corporations and global institutions of governance, like the WTO, IMF, OECD and WB, are seen to be facilitators of the widespread rent-seeking behaviour that has created a global class of rentier elites. One argument goes as far as to say that 'the institutional architecture of rentier capitalism has created a fearsome edifice for siphoning income into the hands of the plutocracy.'[17] Rentier capitalism, according to this view, is therefore an aberration of what capitalism could be and perhaps once was.

Another dimension of the rentier capitalism discourse observes that rents are less an aberration of market ideals and more the logical conclusion of what a 'pure and perfect' market for capital would look like. Rent according to this view, defined as remuneration for ownership of assets rather than a contribution of labour to economic production, will be a feature of any society where capital is privately owned. In such societies, not only is it possible that rentiers can exist, but it is evident that today the creation and capture of rents by the wealthiest in society have generated unprecedented levels of economic inequality. The 'fundamental force of divergence' that explains this current situation can be expressed, according to this view, by the inequality r>g, whereby r represents asset returns and g is real income.[18] Therefore, while some elements of the rentier capitalism thesis emphasize the corruption of capitalist ideals, others suggest that the economic inequality driving rentier capitalism is in fact the logical conclusion of capital markets operating as they should.

One final view to be considered in the rentier capitalism scholarship is that which attributes the problem of rents to monopoly. A recent contribution to this theme puts the issue forcefully, claiming that the essence of rent and thus the key to understanding the rise of rentier capitalism is monopoly, which, 'by providing the conditions under which an asset can generate an income – is the very sea in which the rentier swims'.[19] This approach also eschews the moral critique of rentier capitalism by framing the issue as not one of fairness – i.e., that rentier income is unearned – but rather that when capitalist firms are not subject to the forces of competition – i.e., in the context of monopoly – the single redeeming feature of capitalism, that which drives its essential dynamism, inter-capitalist competition, disappears.[20] According to this account, the economic transformation of the United Kingdom since the 1970s has been understood till now as one of neo-liberalism, with financialization as its leading edge. However, when seen through the lens of this monopoly-oriented notion of rent, it is more appropriate to characterize this overall process as not one of financialized neo-liberalism, but rather of rentierization.[21]

These three prongs of the intellectual assault on rentier capitalism advocate policy responses in the context of social upheavals responding to the worst excesses of a society in which the creation and capture of rents has become endemic. The moral critique proposes the implementation of a social safety net through a universal basic income. Addressing the exponential growth of wealth relative to income would require radical redistributive measures such as a global inheritance tax, according to those who consider rentier capitalism as the result of an ideal market for capital. Reading rent through the lens of monopoly results in demands for an assertive programme of state-led investment and regulation aimed at busting corporate monopoly control of leading sectors of the global economy.

There are clear areas of opportunity alongside imperatives for the study of rent in political economy. Whether it be unpicking the class dimensions of struggle over economic output, mapping and combating unprecedented levels of economic inequality, tackling head on the practical aspects of living with and beating back climate change, or resisting the formation of global plutocracy, rent is a vital consideration in the attempt to demystify the present moment. As the discussion so far has suggested, however, rent is multifaceted and contentious. Even with this very brief and selective survey of the rentier capitalism scholarship, we can see tensions emerging with respect to the diagnosis of the problems and their proposed solutions. Is rentier capitalism an aberration, or corruption, of an ideal, profit-driven and competitive capitalism, or the consequence of it? Are the prospective solutions offered up to these problems at odds? Reasons to study rent abound and are important. So, too, is the need for clarity in how rent is understood.

Concepts and contexts in rent theory

Before discussing some of the key shifts in thinking about rent in their historical context, it is important to reiterate one of the key themes that has been explored throughout the previous chapters. There is no universally accepted definition of rent. What we have, rather, is a handful of approaches to explaining rent that are at odds in important ways. Moreover, the disagreements or contending views on rent lead to very different conclusions about what is to be done about it. The point of this book has not been to convince or to advocate on behalf of a preferred view. There is one – the patterns of accumulation approach used in the SoP framework – but it is of no concern in this current study to stake claims as to its superiority. Rather, the task at hand has been to show that contending views on rent can be understood in relation to how they were conceived and can therefore be evaluated according to how they help explain current social phenomena in conjunction with the other tools of political economic analysis with which they inhere.

There are consequences, for example, of accepting the mainstream definition of rent as applying to all factors of production because of limited supply. The logical distinctions between rent, interest, profit, and wages are compromised and so too are their corresponding explanations in theory. Those critical of the mainstream must therefore deal with these logical problems when adopting such positions on rent but from a different normative vantage point. Again, it is not so much that there is a problem with this approach inherently, but rather that such an issue needs to be dealt with explicitly when constructing ideal notions of how capitalism operates today, such as in the rentier capitalism scholarship. The obverse also holds. Accepting a more obscure and, according to some, outdated perception of rent that views it as a revenue unique to owners of landed property carries with it intellectual baggage. The disassociation with rent from monopoly, for example, means that an alternative explanation for the effects of monopoly must be formulated to explain things that could be grasped through the lens of rent theory in mainstream approaches. Whichever way rent is understood, there are consequences for the way real-world problems today are explained. Economic inequality, economic stagnation, climate change, resource depletion and many other topics of social importance can be unlocked through an examination using rent theory. The point is that each approach has limitations. Sketching these limitations has been the goal of the discussion thus far.

The contest of economic ideas on rent has hinged on these limitations at specific historical moments. At each of these moments, shifts in thinking about rent have been consequences of material changes as well as causes of them. The emergence of liberal trade theory, commonly known as free trade arguments, was bound up in the debates over tariffs on corn, or the Corn Laws debates in the United Kingdom during the nineteenth century. It was these debates that generated contending views on rent theory that cohered as the classical, or Ricardian, theory of rent. In this way, rent can be considered as a key concern in the earliest debates over international trade and the subsequent discourse of globalization that would follow.

Debates on globalization encompass many themes. Is globalization good or bad? This would be the obvious question, to which many have offered answers. The tenor of current disputes over this issue is rather blustery, with 'globalism' taking on something of a sinister character in public discourse since at least 2016, when Brexit and Trump set the stage for a dramatic end to the second decade of the twenty-first century. Perhaps the preceding years of political and economic turbulence since the GFC had a role in shaping the animosity towards globalization that such campaigns were thought to have channelled. Maybe the disaffection with the vision offered up by globalized capitalism has its roots much further back, starting with the collapse of the Soviet Union or with the first Iraq war. Whenever it began, a consistent theme in the critique of globalization is that its benefits are not equally shared and that perhaps its promise of greater prosperity for all involved have not and will not materialize. The vehicle through which this promise is supposed to be carried, or fails, is typically seen to be free trade. The antithesis of globalization is associated with protectionism in some form. 'Make America Great Again' or 'Britain First' are very recent iterations of much older positions in deliberations about trade that reach back to the very beginnings of capitalism. Rent featured prominently in these discussions then, and it does so to this day.

The economic logic to the political arguments for so-called free trade is not difficult to understand. If trade between nations is free, countries would specialize in producing goods and services that they do best, thereby producing more than others would if they tried, meaning that there would be more goods and services overall to go around. The reason countries specialize in producing goods and services in whose manufacture they are most capable is because the money they make from selling them on the world market will be able to fund a higher level of imports. If countries raise barriers to trade through tariffs, however, some will produce goods and services they were not very good at making, drawing resources away from what they are good at, dropping the overall amount of goods and services to be traded. It is, therefore, in the interests of all nations to strive towards a world where trade is as free as possible so that all countries utilize their resources efficiently to produce more goods and services overall.

This argument is supposed to have emerged in the late eighteenth century through the work of people like Adam Smith, someone widely considered to be among the pioneering contributors to the modern discipline of economics. Smith, as has been noted earlier, acts as something of a conduit in the history of economic thought as it relates to rent theory, between the physiocrats and the classical school of political economy. It is typically understood that Smith's critique of mercantilist economic thought, associated with people like Thomas Mun and Jean-Baptiste Colbert who advocated the promotion of trade surpluses with an emphasis on producing manufactured goods, sets the foundation for subsequent claims as to the advantages of free trade and free markets. David Ricardo would take up the assault on mercantilism, advocating for the repeal of the Corn Laws and thereby ushering in a new age of rational and globally oriented economic thinking when it came to issues of trade, competition and rent.

This general trajectory of the free trade argument can be traced through four concepts in the history of economic thought associated with what is known as liberal trade theory: Smith's theory of absolute advantage; Ricardo's theory of comparative advantage; the Heckscher–Ohlin theorem; and the Stolper–Samuelson results. A country has an absolute advantage in the production of goods and services that they can make more of than others with less inputs. Comparative advantage arises when a country can make more of one good or service compared to another, relative to their own stock of resources. The Heckscher–Ohlin theorem is a means to determine what to produce based on the resource mix a country has, and the Stolper–Samuelson results identify who gains from this specialization. The key results of these theories are that countries should specialize in producing goods that are intensive in the use of their abundant factors of production. Furthermore, free trade benefits owners of abundant factors of production while harming owners of scarce ones. The obverse is also true. If Smith and Ricardo's absolute and relative advantage concepts explain why a country should engage in free trade, the Heckscher–Ohlin theorem tells them what to produce and the Stolper–Samuelson results can predict who wins and who loses within the country. Bound up in all of this is an assumption that rent, the payment to landowners for the use of land, acts as a handbrake on social progress because it diverts surplus away from productive use and into the pockets of rentiers.

Free trade arguments articulated in the context of the Corn Laws debates can therefore be understood as an intellectual justification for undermining the political and economic power of landowners. Repealing the Corn Laws and thereby removing the tariff on corn imports meant that grain grown in the colonies in North America could meet the demands for food in Britain without having to rely on the land owned by British landlords. If the demand for grain in Britain could be met by cheap imported products, then there was no reason for farmers to pay landlords rent to cultivate land. Those capitalist farmers could take their money and invest it in other spheres of industry where they could pocket the profits that would have otherwise been paid as rents to landlords.

This historically specific defence of liberal trade arrangements premised on the claim that rent acts as a handbrake on social progress has been refined over the past two hundred years to establish a sophisticated foundation for advocating the benefits of globalization. One prominent version of the pro-globalization – i.e., the integration of the national economy into the world economy – argument offers a taxonomy of the general phenomenon by emphasizing five specific forms: trade, direct foreign investment (multinationals), short-term capital flows (portfolio investment), cross-border flows of humanity, diffusion of technology.[22] The first two are to be encouraged while the last three require more cautious consideration. In other words, goods should be traded freely, and firms should be permitted to operate across borders, but the movement of money, people and technology mediated by patents should be less free in their abilities to move between countries. One of the main reasons for advocating the government should step away from the free operation of the markets is that opportunities for rent seeking would be eradicated. Recall the mainstream concept of rent seeking from chapter 3. If governments created and implemented a system of tariffs, manipulating the prices of imports and exports, firms would be incentivized to devote resources to lobbying governments to minimize competition in their sphere of industry. This (mis)use of resources is unproductive because firms could be using them to make more goods rather than trying to affect the state of competition for their products. In this way, protectionism creates the potential for rent-seeking behaviour and is therefore socially unproductive.

The globalization debate emerged in the nineteenth century in relation to a tariff on grain imports which was about questioning the need for landowners to hold back social progress through their monopoly ownership of land. Over time, as this question of monopoly power and rent has come to apply to more than just land, the notion that rent seeking acts as a handbrake on social progress features prominently in debates over the desirability of free trade. As the consequences of Brexit and the ongoing trade war between China and the United States continue to unfold, the globalization debate, in relation to rents and rent seeking, continues to be relevant and important.

The reframing of Ricardian principles of rent – i.e., rent as a producer surplus, the component of price over and above the cost of production plus average profit – as applying across all factors of production and not just to land was the key contribution of the neoclassical or marginalist revolution from the 1870s. Rent in the neoclassical framework became a signal of markets operating inefficiently, distorted by some exogenous intervention. That governments were a primary source of such distortion in this view became a vital justification for the scaling back of government in the economy. Within a century, the neoclassical view of rent, which had subsumed Ricardian principles, would come to prevail during a broader assault on the state and its capacity to manage the economy. Rent in theory and in practice would become vital to the emergence of what has now been dubbed neo-liberalism. Rent seeking would become synonymous with government inefficiency and corruption while the oil rents generated by the OPEC oil embargoes of 1973 and 1979 would come to fuel dramatic debt increases and associated policy decisions in a fundamental rearticulation of the international division of labour.

The term 'neo-liberalism' would be familiar to most involved in the social sciences. It is one of the three big '-isms' or '-izations' of the past few decades, orienting inquiries into the nature of global capitalism since at least the early 2000s. What exactly is neo-liberalism, and what does rent have to do with it? There are contending views, but the usual narrative goes that sometime in the 1970s there was a shift in the dominant logic of economic policy from something of a state-led regime of demand management pegged to a commitment to full employment to a more laissez-faire approach which emphasized the dangers of inflation and advocated the freeing up of markets. The global economic downturn of the early 1970s was seen to be the catalyst for this change because of the emergence of something called 'stagflation' – i.e., the simultaneous occurrence of inflation and economic stagnation, manifesting namely as high unemployment. This apparently new phenomenon was not supposed to be possible according to the prevailing wisdom in economic thinking at the time, typically associated with the work of John Maynard Keynes. Inflation and unemployment were, according to the depiction of Keynesian thought in the dominant narrative of neo-liberalism, mutually exclusive, whereby as prices in the economy rose, production would increase, calling more resources into work and driving down employment. Or, if unemployment rose, demand for goods and services would decline with a corresponding fall in prices, driving down inflation. This relationship was apparently borne out by evidence in the famous Phillips curve, which showed an inverse relationship between wages and unemployment in the United Kingdom between 1861 and 1957. Stagflation in the 1970s was claimed to be evidence to the contrary and therefore an assault on the orthodoxy of state-led demand management which had been seen to be the underlying policy logic that had sustained the post-war boom, the so-called 'golden age' of capitalism, which was mobilized by dissident economists, politicians and business people broadly considered part of what has been dubbed the 'neo-liberal thought collective'.[23] The consequences of this assault have been well documented. Decades of privatization, deregulation and austerity would ensue, creating the fault lines in the global economy that would one day erupt in the GFC and its subsequent social crises.

Rent, as payment for access to oil to its owners – i.e., the governments of oil-producing countries – features in this story from the very beginning. The contestation over the oil rents during the OPEC oil crises paved the way for the Latin American debt crisis and IMF structural adjustment programmes and the 'Volcker Shock' of 1979. The OPEC oil price 'shock' that resulted from the brief oil embargo of

1973 gave the oil-producing states like Saudi Arabia, Kuwait and Abu Dhabi vast amounts of financial power.[24] So much so, it seems, that the United States was prepared to invade the oil-producing states to ensure supply of oil and to bring down its price, according to British intelligence reports.[25] Saudi Arabia agreed, most likely under threat from the US government, to recycle the proceeds of the oil-price hike through New York-based investment banks.[26] Other OPEC countries did the same and soon the New York investment banks found themselves holding about $450 billion 'petro-dollars' to invest.[27] Most advanced industrial economies at the time were experiencing sluggish growth in the midst of rising inflation, so developing economies represented better prospects for high returns. Economies in South and Central America welcomed the investment of petrodollars, taking on large debts to the New York investment banks. Debt levels in the global South soared, going from around $400 billion in 1970 to $1.6 trillion by 1982. Significant portions of this debt was used to pay for precisely what caused it, rising petrol prices, exacerbated once more in 1979 by the price hike associated with the Iranian revolution. As the loans were issued by New York investment banks, all debts were issued in US dollars, meaning that the debtors were vulnerable to interest rate rises in the United States. When Paul Volcker, the Chair of the Federal Reserve from 1979, began to pursue a programme of 'shock therapy' by increasing interest rates as high as 20%, he drove the US economy into a deep recession but also successfully curbed inflation.[28] The interest rate hikes made repayments impossible for countries in the global South that had taken on large debts to US-based banks. In 1982, Mexico became the first country to default on its debts and this began a series of International Monetary Fund (IMF) interventions known as Structural Adjustment Plans (SAPs). Basically, the IMF would step in to loan money to countries who could not afford to meet their repayments for loans to US-based investment banks. The catch was that the IMF money came with conditions like privatization of public assets, liberalizing trade and financial arrangements and fiscal austerity – the cornerstones of neo-liberalism.

The exact definition of neo-liberalism, whether it is still with us and the scope of its consequences are all contentious issues. There is broad agreement, though, about when it emerges and what its advocates and proselytizers were reacting to. The struggle over oil rents in the 1970s and the consequences of where this surplus ended up played a key role in the emergence of what came to be known as neo-liberalism.

This new neo-liberal global capitalism that emerges from the 1970s is accentuated by the imperatives for money to appear to beget money. The expansion of finance seems to occur without the requisite production of tangible things, as did previous bouts of economic growth. This financialized neo-liberal capitalism, so-called because it appears the financial sector of the economy plays a determinate role in shaping economic growth, corresponds to a period of immense growth in some sectors of the global economy but also of unprecedented levels of economic inequality. The famous r>g, whereby r is asset returns and g is income, helps explain the trend in inequality but also pulls the question of rent, understood broadly in neoclassical terms as revenue for having rather than for doing, back into focus for the social sciences. At each stage of the development of capitalism from the nineteenth century to the twenty-first, rent has figured prominently in attempts to explain what is happening and why. This is, of course, not surprising given rent is a revenue for ownership in a social system where the production, exchange and distribution of resources are mediated by private property rights.

Financial rent is the term given to the economic rent paid to owners of financial assets. This definition derives from the mainstream notion of economic rent and it is also deployed within heterodox scholarship to illuminate the excesses of modern finance. Financialization is arguably the social process most discussed in social science scholarship throughout the past decade as an adjunct to, and in connection with, neo-liberalism and globalization before it. Financial rent seeking is one prominent theme in the literature on financialization which has drawn heavy criticism, especially in the wake of the 2008 GFC.

The Occupy Wall Street movement emerged as a response to what were considered undesirable levels of economic inequality driven by a mode of social organization catering to the needs of financiers and their associates. The slogan 'We are the 99%' captured this sentiment, spotlighting the unfairness but also the untenability of a society in which most people were immiserated to the benefit of a small and powerful elite. The r>g formulation of economic inequality driven by the appreciation of asset values – i.e., the accumulation of wealth – outstripping increases in real incomes for productive labour – i.e., wage rises – emerged as an explanation of the historical trends that the Occupy movement were reacting to. Front of mind for the Occupy protestors was the redistribution of wealth from the many to the few. In the United States, where the Occupy movement began, the income of the top 1% grew from 275% between 1979 and 2007, while those in the bottom 20% saw a mere 18% increase in theirs.[29] This unprecedented level of income inequality underpinned concerns about the lobbying power of corporations and the richest citizens to divert state resources away from the provisioning of needs for most people. Similar concerns were raised by the UNCTAD report, cited above, under the guise of rentier capitalism. Others have called financialization 'profiting without producing',[30] while some have denied financialization occurred at all, claiming that rather what was known as financialization was actually 'rentierization'.[31] It is easy to see how the lines between '-izations' is blurred when rent and profit are rendered ambiguous due to the acceptance of the neoclassical premise of rent as applying to all factors of production. One novel connection between financialization and the more obscure notion of rent as unique to capitalist landed property sees the financialization of mortgages – i.e., the subsumption of mortgage repayments into the logic of interest-bearing capital, or financial industry – as explaining why house prices keep rising in places like the United Kingdom, but housing supply does not increase commensurately.[32] As the investment of money into housing construction confronts the barrier of landed property, landowners can capture some of the money invested into producing more housing stock as rent, thereby driving up the price without calling more housing into production.

The way in which rent is understood directly limits the scope of its capacity to explain social problems and how their solutions might be constructed. This is evident in examples relating to the manifestations of broad social processes like globalization, neo-liberalism and financialization. These considerations are particularly important for considering the future of rent theory in political economy. One example that bears this out in very obvious ways is the contention between what some call financialization – i.e., profiting without producing – and others might call rentierization – i.e., income deriving from having rather than doing. The definitions sound exactly the same but the concepts have profoundly different consequences for how the problems of capitalism are construed and what their solutions might entail.

Is rent really about land or monopoly? This was one of the first questions posed at the start of this book and, while the discussion has covered various topics to do with rent, this issue has not yet been resolved. Such is the state of rent theory today. While there is a resurgence in scholarly and popular interest in rentier capitalism, with its problematic rent-seeking behaviour, economic inequality and largely deleterious social consequences, conceptual coherence on rent seems elusive still. On the one hand, there is a huge body of literature that accepts the view that rents are the function of competition in markets for factors of production. Any influences affecting competition in these markets are therefore potential explanations for the emergence of rents, which are inherently problematic. On the other hand, there is a more obscure view that sees rent as the payment for the use of land in capitalism, whereby historically specific forms of landed property obstruct the passage of investment into land-based commodity production. Moreover, to further complicate the issue, there is a tendency in this approach to treat this obstructive role of rent as an example of monopoly power. That is, rent becomes, as with the competition-based view, a means to explain the causes and consequences of monopoly. It is hoped that the brief foray into the controversies surrounding the formulation of rent theories up to the proliferation of scholarship on rentier capitalism in the present has at least piqued the interest of those keen to understand the present moment. If capitalism with its rentier inflection is to be torn asunder, we must proceed from a strong foundation of conceptual coherence to know what exactly is to be 'rent'.

Notes

Chapter 1 What is Rent?

1 Klein (1966): 1327.
2 Sedgwick (2009): 58.
3 Marshall and Marshall (1881): 144.
4 OECD, 'Housing Market Indicators', accessed 15 April 2021. http://www.oecd.org/housing/data/affordable-housing-database/housing-market.htm
5 OECD, 'Housing Tenures', accessed 15 April 2021. https://www.oecd.org/els/family/HM1-3-Housing-tenures.pdf
6 OECD, 'Population', accessed 15 April 2021. https://data.oecd.org/pop/population.htm
7 Bogdan (2018).
8 Bogdan (2018).
9 Martin, Hulse and Pawson (2018).
10 Shelter Scotland (2018).
11 Jones (2018).
12 Bancroft and Wace (2019).
13 O'Connell (2020).
14 Milne (2020).
15 Aviles (2020).
16 Ibid.
17 Singletary (2020).
18 Williams (2020).
19 Parker and Friedman (2020).
20 Gabbatt (2020).
21 Arena Housing Project, 'Rent Strikes and Housing Activism in Europe during the Coronavirus Crisis', accessed 15 April 2021.

https://maphub.net/JournalismArena/rent-strikes-and-housing-activism-in-europe-during-coronavirus
22 Ponsford (2020).
23 Ponsford (2020).
24 Wall (2020).
25 Ibid.
26 Christophers (2015).
27 Dunn (2017).
28 Christophers (2020): 5.
29 Ibid.: xvii–xviii.
30 Ibid.: xvi.
31 The articles listed here dealing with the Covid-19 pandemic, climate change, inequality and economic crisis respectively, in relation to rent, are cases in point: https://www.theguardian.com/commentisfree/2020/aug/12/ppe-britain-rentier-capitalism-assets-uk-economy; https://foreignpolicy.com/2021/04/06/death-neoliberalism-larry-summers-biden-pandemic/; https://www.forbes.com/sites/rhockett/2021/04/04/the-specter-of-the-specter-of-inflation/?sh=262fbfd915a0; https://www.afr.com/policy/economy/tricks-to-kick-debt-habit-20210325-p57e4b
32 Marx (1981 [1894]): 103.
33 Fine (1983): 133.
34 Ibid.

Chapter 2 Rent Theory in Historical Perspective

1 Ghazanfar (1997): 40–1.
2 Hosseini (2003): 34.
3 Ghazanfar (1997): 41.
4 Rubin (1979): 19.
5 Ibid.
6 Baosan (2014): 59.
7 Dawson (1993).
8 Fox-Genovese (1976): 9.
9 Leshem (2016): 225.
10 Fox-Genovese (1976): 9.
11 Quesnay (1963 [1766]): 231.
12 Théré and Charles (2007): 212.
13 Turgot (1898 [1770]): 46.
14 Orain (2015): 384.
15 Marx (1963 [1862–3]): 45.
16 Ibid.

17 Roll (1992): 120.
18 Meek (1963): 25.
19 Ware (1931): 613.
20 Roll (1992): 111.
21 Meek (1956): 55–7.
22 Smith (1976 [1776]): 364.
23 Wilson (1840): iv.
24 Salvadori and Signorino (2015): 182.
25 Ricardo 1973 [1817]): 33.
26 Ibid.: 46.
27 Ibid.: 46.
28 Ibid.: 33.
29 Ibid.: 5.
30 Malthus (1986 [1820]): 136.
31 Macleod (1986): 96.
32 Mill (1909 [1848]): 422.
33 Ibid.: 422.
34 Ibid.: 422.
35 Ibid.: 423.
36 Ibid.: 141.
37 Marx (1975a): 380.
38 Marx (1975b): 396.
39 Marx (1981 [1894]): 279.
40 Hansman (2017).
41 Fine and Saad-Filho (2016): 147.

Chapter 3 Mainstream Rent Theory

 1 Robbins (1932): 15.
 2 See, for example: Beggs (2011); Lawson (2013): 948; Schumpeter
    (2005 [1932]): 118–19; Colander (2000): 127.
 3 Primrose (2017): 88.
 4 Morgan (2016): 5.
 5 Madra (2016): 71.
 6 'Economics A–Z Terms Beginning with R', *Economist
    Magazine*, accessed 15 April 2021. https://www.economist.com/
    %20economics-a-to-z/r%20%E2%80%93%20node-
    21529784
 7 Ibid.
 8 Alchian (2008): 5508.
 9 Rutherford (2013): 507–8.
10 Butcher (2012).

11 Cooper (2019).
12 Goasduff (2021).
13 'Why is sweet crude oil better than sour crude oil?' *Tank Farm Nigeria*, accessed 15 April 2021. https://www.tankfarmnigeria.com/sweet-crude-oil/
14 Alchian (2008): 5508.
15 Carrington (2015).
16 'Lance Armstrong Net Worth', *Celebrity Net Worth*, accessed 15 April 2021. https://www.celebritynetworth.com/richest-athletes/olympians/lance-armstrong-net-worth/
17 Stilwell (2019): 98.
18 Reuters (2017).
19 'Lance Armstrong net worth'.
20 Krueger (1974): 301–2.
21 Tullock (1967): 232.
22 Fine and Milonakis (2009): 61.
23 Ahmed (2016): 35.
24 Kelsall (2012): 677.
25 Ibid.: 678.
26 Khan (2005): 712.
27 Arrow and Debreu (1954): 265–90.
28 Blaug (2003): 146.
29 Weintraub (1991): 104–7.
30 Blaug (2003): 147.
31 Walker (1997): 91–110.
32 Blaug (2003): 147.
33 Martins (2015): 1110.
34 Fine (1983): 140.

Chapter 4 Rent Theory in Modern Political Economy

1 Stilwell (2015): 8.
2 Gills and Morgan (2020): 12.
3 Arnsperger and Varoufakis (2003, 2006).
4 Fine (2013).
5 Nwoke (1987): 9.
6 Fine (1994): 279.
7 Wilson (2010).
8 Rutherford (2013): 590.
9 Heertje (1977).

10 Birch (2019): 8.
11 Saardchom (2014): 222.
12 Nicas (2018).
13 Thomas (2010): 10.
14 Filomeno (2014): 16.
15 Quadrio-Curzio (2018): 7573–7.
16 Hotelling (1931): 137.
17 Christophers (2020): 1–48.
18 As used in studies of rentier capitalism like Christophers (2020): xxi–xxiii.
19 Fine (1983): 141.

Chapter 5 Why is Rent Important Today?

1 UNCTAD (2017): 119.
2 '#1 Jeff Bezos', *Forbes*, accessed 12 May 2021. https://www.forbes.com/profile/jeff-bezos/?sh=5fbaaf731b23
3 Archyde (2020).
4 Sweney (2020).
5 UN News (2021).
6 UNEP (2021).
7 'How the Footprint Works', *Global Footprint Network*, accessed 13 May 2021. https://www.footprintnetwork.org/our-work/ecological-footprint/
8 Kratena (2008): 514.
9 'A Plan for Transitioning Infrastructure to Net Zero', Institution of Civil Engineers, accessed 27 April 2021. https://www.ice.org.uk/getattachment/news-and-insight/policy/plan-for-transitioning-infrastructure-to-net-zero/ICE_Net-Zero_Infrastructure_Plan_Paper__Final.pdf.aspx
10 CCC (2019).
11 Andreucci, Garcia-Lamarca, Wedekind and Swyngedouw (2017): 31.
12 Ibid.: 40.
13 'Chapter 1. Bourgeois and Proletarians', *Manifesto of the Communist Party,* accessed 27 April 2021. https://www.marxists.org/archive/marx/works/1848/communist-manifesto/ch01.htm#007
14 Christophers (2020): 31.
15 Standing (2017): 24.
16 Ibid.: 24–5.
17 Ibid.: 83.

18 Piketty (2014): 424.
19 Christophers (2020): 29.
20 Christophers (2019): 316–23.
21 Christophers (2020): 5.
22 Bhagwati (2013): 4–5.
23 Mirowski (2009).
24 Harvey (2005): 27.
25 Alvarez (2004).
26 Gowan (1999): 20.
27 Hickel (2017): 150.
28 Dealbook (2019).
29 Van Gelder (2011): 11.
30 Lapavitsas (2013).
31 Christophers (2020): 5.
32 Fine (2010): 106.

References

Ahmed, S. 2016. *Rentier Capitalism: Disorganised Development and Social Injustice in Pakistan*. New York: Palgrave Macmillan.

Alchian, A. A. 2008. 'Rent', in *The New Palgrave Dictionary of Economics, Living Edition*, ed. M. Vernengo, E. P. Caldentey and B. J. Rosser Jr. London: Palgrave Macmillan.

Alvarez, L. 2004. 'Britain Says US Planned to Seize Oil in '73 Crisis'. *New York Times*, 2 January. https://www.nytimes.com/2004/01/02/world/britain-says-us-planned-to-seize-oil-in-73-crisis.html

Andreucci, D., Garcia-Lamarca, M., Wedekind, J. and Swyngedouw, E. 2017. '"Value Grabbing": A Political Ecology of Rent'. *Capitalism Nature Socialism* 28(3): 28–47.

Archyde. 2020. 'How Much Money Jeff Bezos Makes per Minute, Hour, Day'. 25 November. https://www.archyde.com/how-much-money-jeff-bezos-makes-per-minute-hour-and-day/#:~:text=Thus%2C%20because%20of%20how%20his,and%20about%20%20%24%20223%2C000%20per%20minute

Arnsperger, C. and Varoufakis, Y. 2003. 'Toward a Theory of Solidarity'. *Erkenntnis* 59(2): 157–88.

Arnsperger, C. and Varoufakis, Y. 2006. 'What is Neoclassical Economics?' *Post-Autistic Economics Review* 38, article 1: 2–12.

Arrow, K. J. and Debreu, G. 1954. 'Existence of an Equilibrium for a Competitive Economy'. *Econometrica* 22(3) (July): 265–90.

Aviles, Gwen. 2020. 'Landlords are Targeting Vulnerable Tenants to Solicit Sex in Exchange for Rent, Advocates Say'. *NBC News*, 18 April. https://www.nbcnews.com/news/us-news/landlords-are-targeting-vulnerable-tenants-solicit-sex-exchange-rent-advocates-n1186416

Bancroft, Holly and Wace, Charlotte. 2019. 'Exposed: Sex for Rent Landlords who have Tried to Entice 250,000 UK Women into Bed are STILL Advertising Online Despite Threat of Seven-year Jail Sentences'. *Mail on Sunday*, 17 March, https://www.dailymail.co.uk/news/article-6817781/Exposed-Sex-rent-landlords-advertising-online-despite-threat-seven-year-jail-sentences.html

Baosan, Wu. 2014. 'On the Major Fields and Significance of the Study of the History of Ancient Chinese Economic Thought', in Cheng Lin, Terry Peach and Wang Fang (eds), *The History of Ancient Chinese Economic Thought*. London: Routledge.

Beggs, Mike. 2011. 'Zombie Marx'. *Jacobin*, 14 July. https://www.jacobinmag.com/2011/07/zombie-marx

Bhagwati, J. 2013. 'Can We Still Defend Globalization after the Current Crisis?' *Economic Record* 89 (June): 4–5.

Birch, Kean. 2019. 'Technoscience Rent: Toward a Theory of Rentiership for Technoscientific Capitalism'. *Science, Technology & Human Values* 45(1): 3–33.

Blaug, M. 2003. 'The Formalist Revolution of the 1950s'. *Journal of the History of Economic Thought* 25(3): 145–56.

Bogdan. 2018. 'Renting Landscape in 30 Countries around the World'. *RENTcafé*, 12 February. https://www.rentcafe.com/blog/rental-market/renting-landscape-30-countries-around-world/

Butcher, Bryan D. 2012. 'Alaska's Oil and Gas Fiscal Regime'. *Alaska Department of Revenue*, January. https://www.ourenergypolicy.org/wp-content/uploads/2013/09/acloserlook.pdf

Carrington, Damian. 2015. 'Leave Fossil Fuels Buried to Prevent Climate Change, Study Urges'. *The Guardian*, 8 January. https://www.theguardian.com/environment/2015/jan/07/much-worlds-fossil-fuel-reserve-must-stay-buried-prevent-climate-change-study-says

CCC. 2019. 'Net Zero – The UK's Contribution to Stopping Global Warming'. Committee on Climate Change, 2 May. https://www.theccc.org.uk/publication/net-zero-the-uks-contribution-to-stopping-global-warming/

Christophers, Brett. 2015. 'The Limits to Financialization'. *Dialogues in Human Geography* 5(2): 183–200.

Christophers, Brett. 2019. *The New Enclosure: The Appropriation of Public Land in Neoliberal Britain*. London: Verso.

Christophers, Brett. 2020. *Rentier Capitalism: Who Owns the Economy and Who Pays for It?* London: Verso.

Colander, D. 2000. 'The Death of Neoclassical Economics'. *Journal of the History of Economic Thought* 22(2): 127–43.

Cooper, Sabrina. 2019. 'Remember When Linda Evangelista Made Waking Up a Five-Figure Act?' *CR Fashion Book*, 9 May https://www.crfashionbook.com/celebrity/a27409908/linda-evangelista-quote-10000-a-day/

Dawson, R. (ed.) 1993. *Confucius: The Analects*. Oxford: Oxford University Press.

Dealbook. 2019. 'The Legacy of Paul Volcker'. *New York Times*, 10 December. https://www.nytimes.com/2019/12/10/business/dealbook/paul-volcker-death-legacy.html

Dunn, Bill. 2017. 'Against Neoliberalism as a Concept'. *Capital & Class* 41(3): 435–54.

Filomeno, Felipe. 2014. *Monsanto and Intellectual Property in South America*. London: Palgrave Macmillan.

Fine, Ben. 1983. 'The Historical Approach to Rent and Price Theory Reconsidered'. *Australian Economic Papers* 22(4): 132–43.

Fine, Ben. 1994. 'Coal, Diamonds and Oil: Towards a Comparative Theory of Mining?' *Review of Political Economy* 6(3): 279–302.

Fine, Ben. 2010. 'Locating Financialisation'. *Historical Materialism* 18(2): 97–116.

Fine, Ben. 2013. 'Economics: Unfit for Purpose'. *Review of Social Economy* 71(3): 373–89.

Fine, B. and Milonakis, D. 2009. *From Economics Imperialism to Freakonomics: The Shifting Boundaries between Economics and Other Social Sciences*. London: Routledge.

Fine, B. and Saad-Filho, A. 2016. *Marx's Capital*, 6th edn. London: Pluto Press.

Fox-Genovese, E. 1976. *The Origins of Physiocracy: Economic Revolution and Social Order in Eighteenth-Century France*. London: Cornell University Press.

Gabbatt, Adam. 2020. 'Thousands of Americans to Take Part in Biggest Rent Strike in Decades'. *Guardian*, 1 May. https://www.theguardian.com/world/2020/may/01/coronavirus-america-rent-strike-protest

Ghazanfar, S. M. 1997. 'Medieval Islamic Socio-economic Thought: Links with Greek and Latin-European Scholarship'. *Humanomics* 13(3): 33–60.

Gills, Barry and Morgan, Jamie. 2020. 'Teaching Climate Complacency: Mainstream Economics Textbooks and the Need for Transformation in Economics Education'. *Globalizations*: 1–17.

Goasduff, Laurence. 2021. 'Gartner Says Worldwide Smartphone Sales Declined 5% in Fourth quarter of 2020'. *Gartner Newsroom*, 22 February. https://www.gartner.com/en/newsroom/press-releases/2021-02-22-4q20-smartphone-market-share-release

Gowan, P. 1999. *The Global Gamble: Washington's Faustian Bid for World Dominance*. London: Verso.

Hansman, H. 2017. 'Congress Moves to Give Away National

Lands, Discounting Billions in Revenue'. *Guardian*, 20 January. https://www.theguardian.com/environment/2017/jan/19/bureau-land-management-federal-lease

Harvey, D. 2005. *A Brief History of Neoliberalism*. Oxford: Oxford University Press.

Heertje, A. 1977. *Economics and Technical Change*. London: Weidenfield and Nicholson.

Hickel, J. 2017. *The Divide: A Brief Guide to Global Inequality and its Solutions*. London: Windmill Books.

Hosseini, H. S. 2003. 'Contributions of Medieval Muslim Scholars to the History of Economics and their Impact: A Refutation of the Schumpetarian Great Gap', in W. J. Samuels, J. B. Davis and J. E. Biddle (eds), *A Companion to the History of Economic Thought*. Oxford: Blackwell.

Hotelling, H. 1931. 'The Economics of Exhaustible Resources'. *Journal of Political Economy* 39(2): 137–75.

Jones, Harvey. 2018. 'Sex for Rent: The Rogue Landlords Who Offer Free Rooms in Return for "Favours"'. *Guardian*, 2 April. https://www.theguardian.com/money/2018/apr/02/sex-for-rent-accommodation-rogue-landlords-campaign

Kelsall, T. 2012. 'Neo-Patrimonialism, Rent-Seeking and Development: Going with the Grain'. *New Political Economy* 17(5): 677–82.

Khan, Mushtaq. 2005. 'Markets, States and Democracy: Patron–Client Networks and the Case for Democracy in Developing Countries'. *Democratisation* 12(5): 704–24.

Klein, Ernest. 1966. *A Comprehensive Etymological Dictionary of the English Language*. London: Elsevier.

Kratena, Kurt. 2008. 'From Ecological Footprint to Ecological Rent: An Economic Indicator for Resource Constraints'. *Ecological Economics* 64 (3): 507–16.

Krueger, A. O. 1974. 'The Political Economy of the Rent-Seeking Society'. *American Economic Review* 64(3): 291–303.

Lapavitsas, Costas. 2013. *Profiting without Producing: How Finance Exploits Us All*. London: Verso.

Lawson, Tony. 2013. 'What is This 'School' Called Neoclassical Economics?' *Cambridge Journal of Economics* 37: 947–83.

Leshem, D. 2016. 'What Did the Ancient Greeks Mean by *Oikonomia*?' *Journal of Economic Perspectives* 30(1): 225–38.

Macleod, H. D. 1986. *The Elements of Economics, Volume II, Part I, Completing Pure Economics*. New York: D. Appleton and Company.

Madra, Y. M. 2016. *Late Neoclassical Economics: The Restoration of Theoretical Humanism in Contemporary Economic Theory*. New York: Routledge.

Malthus, T. R. 1986 [1820]. *Principles of Political Economy.* Fairfield: Augustus M. Kelley.

Marshall, Alfred and Marshall, Mary Paley. 1881. *The Economics of Industry.* London: Macmillan.

Martin, Chris, Hulse, Kath and Pawson, Hal. 2018. 'The Changing Institutions of Private Rental Housing: An International Review'. *Australian Housing and Urban Research Institute*, January. https://www.ahuri.edu.au/__data/assets/pdf_file/0028/15895/ AHURI_Final_Report_No_292_The_changing_institutions_of_ private_rental_housing_an_international_review.pdf

Martins, N. O. 2015. 'Interpreting the Capitalist Order Before and After the Marginalist Revolution'. *Cambridge Journal of Economics* 39(4): 1109–127.

Marx, K. 1963 [1862–3]. *Theories of Surplus Value: Volume IV of Capital, Part I.* Moscow: Progress Publishers.

Marx, K. 1975a. 'Marx to Engels, 18 June', in K. Marx and F. Engels, *Collected Works, Volume 41, Marx and Engels, 1860–1864.* London: Lawrence and Wishart.

Marx, K. 1975b. 'Marx to Engels, 2 August', in K. Marx and F. Engels, *Collected Works, Volume 41, Marx and Engels, 1860–1864.* London: Lawrence and Wishart.

Marx, K. 1981 [1894]. *Capital: A Critique of Political Economy, Volume Three.* London: Penguin.

Meek, R. L. 1956. *Studies in the Labor Theory of Value.* New York: Monthly Review Press.

Meek, R. L. 1963. *The Economics of Physiocracy: Essays and Translations.* Cambridge: Harvard University Press.

Mill, J. S. 1909 [1848]. *Principles of Political Economy: With Some of their Application to Social Philosophy.* London: Longmans and Green.

Milne, Amber. 2020. '"I Had No Choice": Sex for Rent Rises with Coronavirus Poverty'. *Reuters*, 22 May. https://www.reuters.com/ article/us-britain-housing-harassment-trfn-idUSKBN22X2N7

Mirowski, P. 2009. 'The Neo-liberal Thought Collective'. *Renewal* 17(4): 26–36.

Morgan, Jamie. 2016. 'Introduction: The Meaning and Significance of Neoclassical Economics', in Jamie Morgan (ed.), *What is Neoclassical Economics? Debating the Origins, Meanings and Significance.* London: Routledge.

Nicas, J. 2018. 'Apple and Samsung End Smartphone Patent Wars'. *New York Times*, 27 June. https://www.nytimes.com/2018/06/27/ technology/apple-samsung-smartphone-patent.html

Nwoke, Chibuzo N. 1987. *Third World Minerals and Global Pricing: A New Theory.* London: Zed Books.

O'Connell, Oliver. 2020. 'New York Landlord Caught Offering

Rent-free Accommodation in Exchange for Sex'. *Independent*, 1 May. https://www.independent.co.uk/news/world/americas/sex-rent-landlord-new-york-coronavirus-craigslist-pandemic-a9494626.html

Orain, A. 2015. 'Figures of Mockery: The Cultural Disqualification of Physiocracy (1760–1790)'. *European Journal of the History of Economic Thought* 22(3): 383–419.

Parker, Will and Friedman, Nicole. 2020. 'Rent Strike Planned for May 1 as Pain of Coronavirus Deepens'. *Wall Street Journal*, 27 April. https://www.wsj.com/articles/rent-strike-planned-for-may-1-as-pain-of-coronavirus-deepens-11587988800

Piketty, T. 2014. *Capital in the 21st Century*. Cambridge, MA: Harvard University Press.

Ponsford, Matthew. 2020. 'The Hypocrisy of Europe's Big Corporate Landlords'. *City Monitor*, 28 August. https://citymonitor.ai/fabric/hypocrisy-europes-big-corporate-landlords-5239

Primrose, David. 2017. 'The Subjectification of *Homo economicus* in Behavioural Economics'. *Journal of Australian Political Economy* 80: 88–128.

Quadrio-Curzio, A. 2018. 'Land Rent', in *The New Palgrave Dictionary of Economics*, 3rd edn. London: Palgrave Macmillan.

Quesnay, F. 1963 [1766]. 'General Maxims for the Economic Government of an Agricultural Kingdom', in R. L. Meek (ed.), *The Economics of Physiocracy: Essays and Translations*. Cambridge, MA: Harvard University Press.

Reuters. 2017. '"It Makes Little Sense": View from Frontline of Italy's Broadband War', 29 June. https://www.reuters.com/article/italy-broadband-race-idUSL8N1JJ4DY

Ricardo, D. 1973 [1817]. *The Principles of Political Economy and Taxation*. London: Dent.

Robbins, Lionel. 1932. *An Essay on the Nature and Significance of Economic Science*. London: Macmillan.

Roll, E. 1992. *History of Economic Thought*, 5th edn. London: Faber and Faber.

Rubin, I. I. 1979. *A History of Economic Thought*. London: Ink Link.

Rutherford, D. 2013. *Routledge Dictionary of Economics*, 3rd edn. New York: Routledge.

Saardchom, N. 2014. 'Design Patent War: Apple versus Samsung'. *South Asian Journal of Business and Management Cases* 3(2): 221–8.

Salvadori, N. and Signorino, R. 2015. 'Defense versus Opulence? An Appraisal of the Malthus–Ricardo 1815 Controversy on the Corn Laws'. *History of Political Economy* 47(1): 151–84.

Schumpeter, Joseph A. 2005 [1932]. 'Development'. *Journal of Economic Literature* 43(1) (March): 108–20.

Sedgwick, Fred. 2009. *Where Do Words Come From? A Dictionary of Word Origins*. London: Continuum.

Shelter Scotland. 2018. 'Sex for Rent in Scotland: Topic Briefing'. November. https://assets.ctfassets.net/6sqqfrl11sfj/Ms0Qu5JNhsCyoiON3KNes/fbef4353d596b9c5b804c8dfd6bd1bc7/FINAL_Sex_for_rent_in_Scotland_Topic_Briefing.pdf

Singletary, Michelle. 2020. 'FAQ: Rent Strikes during the Pandemic'. *Washington Post*, 8 May. https://www.washingtonpost.com/business/2020/05/07/rent-strike-faq/

Smith, A. 1976 [1776]. *An Inquiry into the Nature and Causes of the Wealth of Nations*. New York: Oxford University Press.

Standing, G. 2017. *The Corruption of Capitalism: Why Rentiers Thrive and Work Does Not Pay*. London: Biteback.

Stilwell, Frank. 2015. 'Heterodox Economics and Political Economy'. *Journal of Australian Political Economy* 75: 5–10.

Stilwell, Frank. 2019. *The Political Economy of Inequality*. Cambridge: Polity Press.

Sweney, Mark. 2020. 'UK and Europe Renew Calls for Global Digital Tax as US quits Talks'. *Guardian*, 18 June. https://www.theguardian.com/media/2020/jun/18/uk-europe-global-digital-tax-us-quits-talks-tech

Théré, C. and Charles, L. 2007. 'François Quesnay: A "Rural Socrates" in Versailles?' *History of Political Economy* 39(1): 195–214.

Thomas, K. 2010. *Investment Incentives and the Global Competition for Capital*. New York: Palgrave Macmillan.

Tullock, G. 1967. 'The Welfare Costs of Tariffs, Monopolies and Theft'. *Economic Inquiry* 53(3): 224–32.

Turgot, A. R. J. 1898 [1770]. *Reflections on the Formation and Distribution of Riches*. New York: Macmillan.

UN News. 2021. 'SDGs Will Address "Three Planetary Crises" Harming Life on Earth'. UN News, 27 April. https://news.un.org/en/story/2021/04/1090762

UNCTAD. 2017. 'Beyond Austerity: Towards a Global New Deal'. *Trade and Development Report 2017*, UNCTAD, 14 September, 119. https://unctad.org/system/files/official-document/tdr2017_en.pdf

UNEP. 2021. 'Executive Summary', *Making Peace with Nature: A Scientific Blueprint to Tackle the Climate, Biodiversity and Pollution Emergency*, 27 April. https://www.unep.org/resources/making-peace-nature

van Gelder, Sarah. 2011. *This Changes Everything: Occupy Wall Street and the 99% Movement*. New York: Berrett-Koehler Publishers.

Walker, D. A. 1997. *Advances in General Equilibrium Theory*. Cheltenham: Edward Elgar.

Wall, Tom. 2020. '"We Won't Be Cash Cows": UK Students Plan the Largest Rent Strikes in 40 Years'. *Guardian*, 6 December, https://www.theguardian.com/education/2020/dec/06/we-wont-be-cash-cows-uk-students-plan-the-largest-rent-strike-in-40-years

Ware, N. J. 1931. 'The Physiocrats: A Study in Economic Rationalization'. *American Economic Review* 21(4): 607–19.

Weintraub, E. R. 1991. *Stabilizing Dynamics: Constructing Economic Knowledge.* Cambridge: Cambridge University Press.

Williams, Dima. 2020. 'May 1 Rent Strike through the Lens of Organisers, Landlords and Industry Leaders'. *Forbes*, 1 May. https://www.forbes.com/sites/dimawilliams/2020/05/01/may-1-rent-strike-through-the-lens-of-organizers-landlords-and-industry-leaders/?sh=3e21c6767b85

Wilson, J. 1840. *Influences of the Corn Laws, as Affecting All the Classes of the Community, and Particularly the Landed Interests*, 2nd edn. London: Longman, Orme, Brown, Green and Longmans.

Wilson, P. 2010. 'Rio's Albanese Uses Rudd Example as a Warning to Other Governments'. *The Australian*, 10 July. http://www.theaustralian.com.au/business/rios-albanese-uses-rudd-example-as-a-warning-to-other-governments/story-e6frg8zx-1225890000530

Index